Powder-blue boxes of Devon's main grandstand have housed Philadelphia society since 1923.

Exercise on the longe line works out the kinks.

(*Overleaf*) Straight from a fairytale, Susan Saltonstall's green wagonette, drawn by matched Welsh ponies, wins the Devon Carriage Marathon.

A WEEK DOWN IN DEVON

Christopher S. Hyde
with photographs by
Joseph F. Viesti *and*
Alan D. Freedman

A WEEK DOWN
A History of the

IN DEVON
Devon Horse Show

Chilton Book Company
Radnor, Pennsylvania

Manufactured in the United States of America

Library of Congress Catalog Card Number: 76-3102
ISBN 0-8019-6458-X

1 2 3 4 5 6 7 8 9 0   5 4 3 2 1 0 9 8 7 6

Contents

Acknowledgments

"His face, in repose, had the sadness of one habituated to the boundless unreliability of horses"

—Anthony Powell
A Dance to The Music of Time

And of writers about horses. The difficulty in describing an institution with the traditions of the Devon Horse Show is the wealth of material that must be omitted. I regret that there was insufficient space to mention all of those who have made Devon what it is today, nor to enumerate all of the champions who have competed there. It may be some consolation that the author feels their absence as much as anyone.

I would like to thank all of those who rifled their attics for old programs and photographs, spent hours answering questions, and otherwise assisted in the preparation of this book:

Mr. John Burkholder; Mrs. Stanley Clader; Mr. Henry L. Collins, III; Mr. Raymond Cox; Mrs. J. Austin duPont; Mr. James Fallon; Mrs. Jane Gordon Fletcher; Mr. and Mrs. Charles L. Harper; Mr. John J. Hill, III; Mrs. L. Norton Hunt; Mrs. Philip L. Lee; Mrs. Clarence J. Lewis, Jr.; Mr. Richard E. McDevitt, Esq. (and his daughter Todd); Mrs. James F. Mitchell, Jr.; Miss Charlotte Ives Montgomery; Mr. and Mrs. James K. Robinson, Jr.; Mrs. Edgar Scott; Mrs. Robert L. Stevens; Mr. Ward Sullivan; the New Bolton Center of the University of Pennsylvania and all of the members of the Horse Show and Country Fair committees who provided both information and encouragement. Mr. Wilmer Fronheiser was also very helpful in providing technical information about the grounds and their care.

The authenticity of *A Week Down in Devon* is due to their assistance. Any errors or ommissions are my own.

Christopher S. Hyde

vii

A WEEK DOWN IN DEVON

Prior to World War I, ringside parking was about equally divided between coaches and horseless carriages. An umbrella, always a wise accessory at Devon, could also serve as a parasol.

The Devon Horse Show:

1896–1975

The Pennsylvania Railroad completed its main line from Philadelphia to Pittsburgh in 1852. By the time the Civil War had ended, the railroad and a related enterprise, the Baldwin Locomotive Works, had already begun to make many Philadelphia fortunes.

During the last decades of the century, the *Pennsy*, rich but not complacent, had begun to investigate ways to increase its profitable passenger traffic. One way was to attract people to new places accessible by rail. The Main Line, formerly a bucolic landscape populated mainly by Welsh farmers, was just such an artificial Eden.

By a judicious combination of pressure, incentive and example, the railroad induced its executives and, later, the wealthy, the near wealthy, and the would-be wealthy to move into one of the nation's first suburbs: a narrow strip bordering the tracks and convenient to its gingerbread stations from Wynnewood to Paoli. Some of its Welsh-sounding names, such as Radnor (formerly Morgan's Corner), Bryn Mawr and Wynnewood, far from being indigenous, were dreamed up in a country-life fantasy that would have done credit to Disney.

The colony took root and soon began to rival Chestnut Hill as the prestigious place to live, especially if one's business affairs were conducted in center city Philadelphia.

The railroad continued its campaign, building huge inns at Bryn Mawr and Devon to attract the summer resort traffic. Many visitors to these resorts decided to build permanent homes and the population of the Main Line continued to rise. By 1890, most of the very wealthy lived on large estates away from the more crowded areas near the tracks, but also far from the convenient transit system that had led them to settle there in the first place.

They solved the local transportation problem with the most elegant assortment of equipages ever to grace an American village. Consider, just for an instant, what it must have been like to roar punctually up to Devon in a plush car with walnut appointments, behind a gigantic Baldwin locomotive snorting steam like a dragon that owned the earth, and to descend to a polished black George IV phaeton with two high-stepping Hackneys driven by your faithful groom. Then consider the meaning of progress.

Of course, most people walked to their homes. But there must have been lines of phaetons and doctors' gigs and hansoms and buckboards and jaunting cars and what have you: an array which can still be seen at the Devon Carriage Marathon. Then came the Devon energy crisis of the late nineteenth century: not enough good horses to go around.

In 1896, the horse was the only form of land transportation, except for the railroad and the bicycle. Horses drew the vans that delivered eggs, milk, butter, bread, newspapers, ice, mail and meat to the door; they hauled the freight and the commuters to the railroad depot. New York, for instance, had a horse population of *one million* at the turn of the century.

The Main Line inhabitants sometimes tended to imitate the British landed gentry, thus the horse also provided the primary source of sport in the form of fox hunting, driving and polo. Racing was still considered a bit too flashy. Polo, however, after its introduction in New York in 1876, caught on rapidly; indeed, the first Devon Horse Show was held in 1896 on the grounds of a polo field.

The people on the Main Line needed horses, especially Saddlebreds and Hackneys for driving, and the supply was limited. Transporting horses by rail was hazardous and expensive, so the accepted way to increase the supply was to encourage local farmers to breed more and better animals.

What better way to encourage local farmers to breed superior animals than a horse show? A horse show open to everyone, with lots of breeding classes, not only for the elegant animals that drove Papa to the station or carried him in the hunting field, but also for heavy draft horses, Clydesdales and Percherons, that were the farmers' pride. (A Clydesdale-Hackney mix also made a good heavy coach horse.)

So the gentry got together one night in the Devon Inn and formed the Devon Horse Show Association. They elected Henry T. Coates president, Lemuel C. Altemus and Henry Mather Warren vice presidents, E. W. Twaddell secretary and David B. Sharp treasurer. In addition to the officers, C. Davis English, J. W. Patter, A. B. Coxe and R. Penn Smith served on the executive committee.

They decided upon July 2 as the date for a one-day show, with entries closing June 27. To avoid conflict with the Philadelphia Horse Show at St. Martin's Green (Wissahickon), the show was held one month later than its present date.

The First Show

July 2 dawned fair. Exhibitors, judges and spectators turned out—there is even a list of those who *watched*—and the Devon Horse Show was launched.

For that time and place, it appears to have been a fairly democratic affair. The largest number of entries, ten, was in Class 14, "Best Roadster Owned by a Farmer." For a one-day show, the first Devon had the impressive number of thirty classes and well

Under the awning, about 1913. These boxes were replaced by the present main grandstand in 1923. In the ring is a class for short-tailed saddle horses, no longer seen at Devon.

over one hundred entries. Although the classes were small, one wonders how all of them were worked in from 9 A.M. until dark, there being only one ring and three judges.

The first show reflected the goals of its originators, with a good number of breeding classes for "Stallions Suitable for Getting the General Purpose Horse"; "Brood Mares with Foal at Foot"; "Yearling Colts and Fillies," both light and heavy-harness types; "Hackney Brood Mares"; "Standard Bred Trotting or Pacing Stallions"; "Hackney Mares with Foal at Foot" and so on. In later years, the "Mare and Foal" class held on Memorial Day became one of the principal attractions of the show, especially for children.

That July 2 also foretold the unusually broad mixture of classes that was to characterize Devon for the next eighty years. Harness horses, Saddlebreds, Hackneys and hunters competed in roughly equal numbers. The show also had a good number of classes for ponies, a feature that evolved into the huge children's crusade that now marks the first two days of Devon. Nor were the ladies left out; they competed in both riding and driving classes. Of course, the ladies rode sidesaddle—a tradition that was not broken until about 1915.

There were none of the now-popular open jumping classes. The sport had only recently originated in Paris and regular working hunters were expected to jump 5 foot obstacles as a matter of course. Hunter class fences at later shows were not only high enough to give a present-day entrant pause, but also included a ghastly assortment of *wire*, hog pens, real brush and sharp picket fences that would make the owner of a conformation hunter gasp in horror. However, the Devon prototype included only an exhibition class over fences, the last of the day, in which five lightweight hunters competed.

All in all, the first day went extremely well. A reporter's comment might apply just as well today as in 1896: "The judges did their work well and promptly and their awards

3

Children's classes have always been an important feature of Devon. Now the driving classes are left to adults.

evidently gave entire satisfaction to the spectators if not the exhibitors."

Insofar as can be determined, the 1896 show was held on the present grounds. There was a fence around the ring, adjacent to the field of the Devon Polo Club, a gazebo in the center of the ring for the judges and officials, a few jumps stacked outside the ring to be set up as needed by the boys of the Normal School—and little else. Spectators came on bicycles, in horse-drawn carriages or on foot, and stood around the ring. Others brought lawn chairs and sat in comfort, shaded from the July sun by pastel parasols, the ladies in crinolines and shirtwaists, the men in vested suits and boaters.

From 1898 to 1900, the show was moved to the lawn of the Devon Inn to increase attendance. One suspects that the railroad had a hand in the move, devised so that its

summer resort guests could watch from the porch.

After 1900 the show simply vanished, not to reappear until 1910. No one knows why. A combination of circumstances seems the most logical explanation. First, most of the well-to-do population of Philadelphia vanished to Northeast Harbor and parts of the Jersey Shore after May 30. Second, the Philadelphia Horse Show at St. Martin's Green was large and flourishing. Finally, the original show did not have an "angel," the *deus ex machina* who has always appeared at the right time with devotion, energy and money—a Thomas Ashton, a William T. Hunter, a Beale or a Clothier—and catalyzes the efforts of all those who make Devon work.

The Horse Show Blue Book, listing the results of all the major shows in the United States, first appeared in 1907. It did not men-

Devon, for onlookers, has always been a place to see and be seen.

tion Devon at all until 1911, when it listed the results of the 1910 show. In the volume in which Devon first appeared, the Philadelphia Horse Show was missing. In 1910, Devon had assumed both the time period—the last week in May—and the bulk of the exhibitors of the Philadelphia show. It kept, however, its old location next to the polo field, convenient to the Devon Inn. And it kept its eclectic mixture of classes and emphasis on breeding.

The 1910 Revival

The defunct one-day show rose from the ashes a giant. It suddenly had everything going for it—general prosperity, ideal timing as the last social event of the spring season, a good location with convenient transportation, and a group of directors who could afford to finance its inevitable losses out of their own pockets.

The Main Line was at the peak of its horsey days, before the war, the automobile and the depression took their toll. It was the heyday of the close-in hunts, Radnor and Rose Tree. W. Plunket Stewart was just beginning to develop the beautiful fox hunting country around Unionville, southwest of West Chester, and Pierre Du Pont's Longwood was the site of hunt breakfasts. A new generation of superb, if sometimes reckless, horsemen and women were trying their luck on the old show circuit from Upperville, Virginia, to Rochester, New York. And the great stables produced champions in an abundance to rival those of Europe.

The style and caliber of riding had also changed. An obscure Italian cavalryman, Federico Caprilli, had developed a new method of cross-country riding which took the world by storm at the Turin Internationale of 1902. Lida Fleitman Bloodgood, one of the finest sidesaddle riders of the time, was the leading exponent of *il sistema* in the United States. Her example and the teaching of Caprilli's disciple, Carlo Santini, brought the message to the colonies; after 1910, just about everyone at Devon rode with his or her own version of what became known as the "forward seat."

The atmosphere had changed too, veering from rusticity to brilliance. Here is a description of the pre-1900 affair: "Although the Devon Show is a very interesting event to the society people who love horses, its original purpose was to encourage the farmers to breed proper stock for riding and driving, coaching, hunting and polo playing. . . . The turnout of young ladies, little misses, and young masters was remarkable and the skill they displayed in riding and driving bespeaks wonderful improvement in the general average of adult horsemen and horsewomen a few years hence."

Devon was already large at the time of its revival in 1910. By 1914, with 1000 entries, it was the largest outdoor show in the United States and very probably in the world. This astounding success was largely due to the efforts of one man: William T. Hunter.

Mr. Hunter owned a farm near the grounds, and his farm office served as the office of the show. He also turned his own horses out to pasture so that exhibitors beyond hacking distance could board their horses for the four days of the show. Since the show had no stable facilities, those from far away had to put up at local farms or the stables of the Devon Inn. Most exhibitors, however, rode or drove to Devon early in the morning, showed in their classes and rode home again at night. It was still a local affair, in spite of having become a society event. Of the 1000 entries in 1914, only one New York stable exhibited.

Mr. Hunter began the tradition of open-

When cars were automobiles. The ladies are studying the results in The Evening Bulletin, *one of the few Philadelphia papers to have survived the intervening years.*

The winner in a pre World War I Hackney class, the prestige event of Devon's early days.

In the beginning was the Railroad. The Pennsy promoted Devon heavily. You can still get there on the Penn Central.

PENNSYLVAN

Frequent Trai

PHOTO BY REILY & WAY, PHILA.

DEVON HO

C. LONG
ral Manager

P. ANDERSON
Passenger Agent

MAY 27, 28

IA RAILROAD

n Service to the

ORSE SHOW
29, 31, 1915

GEO. W. BOY
Passenger Traffic M

D. N. BELL
General Passenger

handed hospitality that continues to make Devon a favorite of exhibitors. But he did not serve merely as a gracious host. He took entries, directed the grounds crew, designed courses, arranged for judges, veterinarians and blacksmiths, established new classes, settled disputes, assigned boxes, kept results, wrote the publicity and sent out clipping books to all exhibitors.

In addition to Mr. Hunter's prodigious efforts, many other families have given continuous support to the show throughout its history. "It wouldn't be Devon without a Cassatt," said Mrs. Thayer, a granddaughter of railroad president Alexander Cassatt, being interviewed in her box at Devon in 1950. Quite right she was, too. But she might have added "or without an Ashton or a Montgomery, or a Du Pont, or a Collins, or a Biddle, or a Coxe. . . " The list is long. Even more unusual than the cross section of Philadelphia society represented at Devon before the war is the continuity of its makeup through almost eighty years. The fourth generation of many of the original families now manages and shows at Devon.

The year of revival, 1910, also was the first year of the Devon box. There were forty-six of them. A canvas awning over the boxes replaced the parasols of a more casual day and sheltered the wife of future governor Earle; the Van Rensselaers and the Du Ponts; Horace Binney Hare; Ellen Mary Cassatt, niece of the painter; a novelist, later ambassador to Russia under FDR, William C. Bullitt; America's first tennis star, William J. Clothier; Frederick W. Schmidt, Philadelphia's most outstanding benefactor; and J. Gardner Cassatt, nephew of Alexander and Mary.

If one looks at the same box numbers today, the names may have changed but it is a safe bet that the present holder is a direct or a collateral descendant of the original occupant. You do not buy a box at Devon unless a new grandstand is built. You inherit it.

Alexander Cassatt had imported one of the first Hackney ponies in the United States. By 1910, the flashy, high-stepping little creatures, along with their big brothers the Hackneys—the horse on the Devon seal is a Hackney—made up some of the most popular classes at Devon. The best known of these, the sire of a notable line, was Willisbrook Farm's Tissington Amity. (Willisbrook farm belonged to Charles E. Coxe and Willisden farm to A. B. Coxe, his brother.)

The art of sidesaddle riding declined steadily after 1915. In today's recently revived classes, the riders no longer even post and the spectators cheer if one of them is able to clear a 3-foot obstacle—a very short-lived sport, since the sidesaddle was invented during the reign of Queen Anne.

During the thirties, one of the sporting columns carried a good-natured debate between Mrs. J. Austin Du Pont, advocate of the sidesaddle, and another brilliant horsewoman who rode astride (then termed *crosssaddle*)—Helen Hope Montgomery, now Mrs. Edgar Scott. The argument was never settled since both of them were capable of jumping a 6-foot wall with equal aplomb. Both are still active at Devon, Mrs. Du Pont as a noted exhibitor of Welsh ponies and Mrs. Scott as Executive Vice-president and Chairman of the Horse Show Committee.

All in all, Mr. Hunter, chairman from 1913 until 1916, was justified in calling Devon the finest outdoor show in the country. He had also seen to the amenities. In front of the four new grandstands with their awnings was a boardwalk to keep the feet of ladies and gentlemen dry in the downpours that traditionally flood at least one day of Devon. The main ring in front of the grandstands was surrounded with a whitewashed panel fence, and in its center was a pillared pavilion to shelter judges and officials. On the north end of the boardwalk was the bandstand, where hard-working musicians in full uniform performed the duties now assumed by an electric organ.

South of the main ring was a slightly smaller one, also fenced in, for schooling. The three sides of the main ring not occupied by grandstands were reserved for carriages and automobiles, beginning a custom of ringside parking that has survived to cause untold grief for subsequent managers.

The grounds themselves were a giant park, almost flat, with closely cropped turf shaded by old trees. There were no buildings at all in the vicinity, except for the Devon Inn whose towers could be seen looming over the trees just to the southeast of the grandstand.

Although the show had no permanent stabling until after World War I, Mr. Hunter had standardized the prices of stabling in the area and arranged for feed to be available on the grounds. One could stable a horse, including both hay and grain, for $3 a day, a price no doubt considered exorbitant at the time.

The outside course, which was to be a feature of Devon for forty-five years, was not set up until after World War I, when hunters began to displace Hackneys and Saddlebreds as the best-filled classes. Not that hunters were lacking before and during the war. There was a large number of classes, even more finely divided than they are today, with light, medium and heavyweight hunters in both men's and women's divisions. Some of the events might be popular if revived today—the hunt teams, for example, in one of which a team of four hunters had to jump six brush fences abreast. A hunter team today consists of three horses and usually only one fence is jumped abreast.

The jumping classes were mostly for green hunters (less than two years show experience). Considering the size of the hunter obstacles in those days, the qualification was apparently no hindrance. In 1916, Skyscraper and Confidence, owned by George Chipchase, tied in the jumper class at a height of 6 feet, 9 inches. In this particular class the object was to get over the fence. Touches didn't count, as they did in AHSA jumper classes; the top rail in high jump classes was sometimes secured with ropes held by handlers on each side of the fence.

Other events no longer seen included the broad jump, over water or stacked cardboard boxes. Harry D. Halloway's Brandon Lass, a pony, standing only 13.2 hands, took second by clearing 23 feet over water in 1914. A whole series of military events was instituted, open to Army officers only, following the European tradition. There were also many breeding classes for heavy draught horses, mostly Percherons, Belgians, and later, Clydesdales, as well as a number of events, including races, for polo ponies.

An Excess of Asceticism

In spite of the flourishing state of the show, there was, as they said, a war on. While it was still an affair of decadent Europeans it could be ignored, but when our boys went over to straighten things out it became serious. Sauerkraut suddenly became "liberty cabbage." The sporting journals sprouted articles by retired colonels demonstrating that horse shows were essential to the maintenance of a strong cavalry, the striking arm of the Army (they were still saying it in 1942). Mr. Busch, grandfather of Augustus Busch who showed in 1975 at Devon, was forced to change the label on his beer from

11

The Smith family at Devon. Boardwalk in front of the stands protected spectators from mud.

Judging the children's pony class. Women organized and judged all children's events.

the German Imperial Eagle to one that looked more like Uncle Sam's. But all to no avail. In an excess of asceticism that eventually led to prohibition, Devon was cancelled in 1918.

It bounced back stronger than ever in 1919 but things had changed. Dr. Thomas B. Ashton, who would be an officer of the show until 1932, was chairman, and the organization was now called The Devon Horse Show and Country Fair. Dr. Ashton's Wynnewood is the Hackney on the Devon seal.

A small symbol of the change that overcame Devon: from 1910 to 1918, the horse's head on the show ribbons faced right; after 1918 it faced left, and the ribbons no longer had white kid backs. Devon would now have a *purpose*; it was time to shed frivolity. Many of the officers of the show were also on the board of the Bryn Mawr Hospital, and they decided that Devon would benefit the hospital. The Devon Horse Show and Country Fair was incorporated and its shareholders bought the grounds and facilities outright.

Unfortunately, the horse show itself had never made a profit. It depended upon the fortunes of its officers and, for a while, on those of a group of rich shareholders to make up the annual deficit. A top-drawer show with permanent facilities, good management, first-class judges and superior hospitality to exhibitors still cannot make a profit today. The current show, with 40,000 paying spectators, is lucky to break even.

Enter Mrs. Archibald Barklie, wife of the Horse Show's vice president. She organized the Country Fair, which has been making increasing contributions to the hospital ever since. The Country Fair, as important a social institution in its own way as the show, will be described in detail in Part Eight. Its Country Village first made an appearance in 1919 and hasn't changed much since. Its board has also remained *the* social club of the Main Line.

At the canter in an early equitation class.

Devon women have always been able to ride or drive anything on four legs. Classes for roadsters like this one were primarily speed events.

Winner in a Devon police competition of the 'teens looks capable of handling any crowd Philadelphia could whip up.

The official photographer of 1913 seemed more interested in cars than horses—automobiles were more of a rarity.

The Village was the first structure of a building boom at Devon that during the twenties would take up much of the tree-lined expanse of the old grounds. William Du Pont, Jr. built the first of the permanent stables, the creosoted wooden barns that still stand northeast of the Wanamaker Oval. Other large exhibitors followed suit, using the same style of building, until eventually the barns formed two sides of a square enclosing the ring and outside course on the east and south. The outside course for hunters, with its fences, stone walls, water and bank jumps, was also completed, surrounding the schooling area between the main ring and the row of barns. In 1923, the four awning-covered grandstands were replaced by a single permanent stand, today's main grandstand. While it covered only a fraction of the former length, more depth and height gave it even greater capacity.

Moving the judges' stand to the northern end of the ring, now occupied by the committee stand, put the final touch on what was to be the essential plan of the Devon grounds for the next forty years.

The year 1921 was something of a watershed. The show was not only officially recognized—it was one of the founding members of the American Horse Shows Association (AHSA) in 1917—but had become an indispensable part of the great eastern show circuit that included the National, Springfield, Long Branch, Rochester and other shows that are now history. There were 174 classes and almost 1500 entries; although there still was a preponderance of Philadelphia-area entries, the great stables from Chicago to Boston, those that exhibited at Madison Square Garden, had "discovered" Devon.

The man who represents Devon in the eyes of exhibitors and the public may be a director, an executive, or one who, like Manager Tom Clark, is not listed as an officer at all. Clark, the guiding spirit of Devon from 1919 to 1942, was an ardent fox hunter and inveterate cigar smoker. A large man, always looking slightly rumpled in the best Devon tradition, he was not above rolling up the legs of his trousers, when the mud of the showgrounds got too deep. When complimented on his management of the show, he replied "I ought to be good with horses, I was born in a barn."

Clark exemplifies a side of Devon that an official history—with its records of the rich, the famous and the socially prominent—tends to neglect. The show is a family affair. It has always had a place for the small local exhibitor, whether he is showing a draft horse, his favorite hunter, or the horse that pulls the family buggy. When professionalism tends to crowd the individual from one type of class—say open jumping—a new one is created to allow him to compete. And there is a certain rough democracy among exhibitors, especially when they get together to commiserate with each other about the judging, the footing, the fences or the latest AHSA ruling. They tend to stick together. Maybe it's a throwback to the days when every man who owned a horse was automatically a cavalier.

The next ten years were relatively uneventful. There was a slight drift toward a preponderance of hunter classes (there were eighty-nine hunters in one class in 1923) at the expense of Hackneys and Saddlebreds— toward brilliance, perhaps, rather than elegance, though the Hackney ponies have continued their eminence to the present day.

In 1923 the show acquired the "yard of tin" that Honey Craven blows to announce the classes: the horn of the coach belonging to the British 16th Lancers.

In 1924 Calvin Coolidge put in an ap-

Thomas W. Clark, general manager of Devon in the Thirties, on a favorite hunter.

Aerial view of Devon during the roaring twenties. The automobile has taken over.

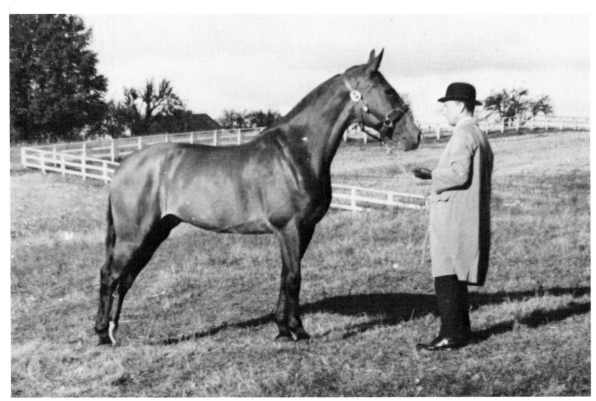

Hunter Billy King after a hard season. Field hunters were also show hunters prior to World War II.

The evolution of show jumping. Early jumping classes were usually filled with hunters, and the typical seat was a cross between the old "legs in front" style and the modern forward seat.

Devilish thoughts before the lead-line class during Devon's junior weekend.

"I think dressing properly always adds to the sport."

The Valley Forge Military Academy mounted drill team performs under the lights.

Elizabeth Lewis exhibits grace and precision of dressage.

Robin Rost, Devon's best child rider in 1975, looks for the next fence.

Robin climbs a triple spread on Wigg's Bar during a junior jumper event.

Palominos, rare in the show ring, can jump too.
This is Feature Farm's Apollo.

A fine day for fine harness horses, on the outside Mrs. Alan Robson's Southern Lullaby.

An elegant pair of Hackneys steps out. Imp. Bonnie Lyn Brocklyn and Imp. Centenial Superlative.

Harness vehicles get almost as much grooming as horses ... but they don't need shoes.

(*Opposite*) Single pony roadster trophy winner Wild Mustard has an action
that practically gives off sparks.

Class. Rodney Jenkins guides show ring aristocrat San Felipe through
regular working hunter appointments class.

Form over fences. Graffiti in a Corinthian class.

Noted hunter rider Dave Kelly has placed Royal Reveler perfectly for low clean flight.

A closer approximation to the modern forward seat in jumping. Victor Sifton on Brian Boru in 1935.

pearance with show secretary Edward Ilsey. He is not recorded to have said anything. Until recently, governors of Pennsylvania always attended Devon as a matter of course on Governor's Day, following Pony Day, Hackney Day and Hunter's and Jumper's Day. Edward F. Beale, president of Pennsylvania Salt Company, became president of Devon in 1924, a post he was to hold until 1942.

Beale's photograph makes him look every inch the Philadelphian of the old school. He rode with the Radnor Hunt, jumping fences until he was eighty-five. The next year, he was bucked off his riding horse, startled by a train whistle. He is quoted as saying from his hospital bed: "Everybody has to grow old but dammit, I don't want to."

In 1928 there were 2000 entries. Since the show lasted only five days and there were no classes at night, the judging, even allowing for the simultaneous classes inside the ring and out, must have been a miracle of efficiency.

Many Main Line families were not as hard hit by the depression as their less fortunate contemporaries. Speculation, whether on the stock market or in theology, has never been socially acceptable in Philadelphia, and though some families had fallen on hard times, few were ruined. The show, somewhat reduced in terms of exhibitors and spectators, went on.

Elizabeth Grinnell, a horsewoman, and writer of flawless prose for *The Sportsman*, wrote in 1931: "Devon did not have as many

21

entries this year, and it was difficult to say whether this was due to financial depression or to the depression that some exhibitors contract when they meet the competition this show presents."

Devon survived intact, however, and by 1936 Mrs. Grinnell could report, "Good as it was in the old days, it is now practically perfect." The classes were once again well filled, the audiences were large and enthusiastic and even the weather cooperated, a rare occurrence for Devon. If there is an abiding presence at Devon, it is the mud. An old quip ran: "In case of sunshine, entry fees will be refunded." Riders made a game of it.

It was in 1936 that the outside course for hunters was altered to run clockwise instead of counterclockwise, eliminating an awkward turn into a stone wall that had marked the earlier course.

Sir Clifford Sifton and Iron Man took the Geist Trophy home to Canada that year, having won two legs on it in 1934 and 1935. A little later, to the dismay of other exhibitors, he also took home what was supposed to have been a perpetual trophy. The owner got tired of adding rings to its bottom each year—after a decade it looked like a laminated wood lamp—and told Sir Clifford to keep it.

The years between 1936 and 1941 saw a brief Indian summer of showing as preparations for war in Europe accelerated. In 1938, the Reich sent thirty officers to Devon, introduced by the German Ambassador, Hans Heinrich Dieckhoff.

In 1939, the great Wanamaker Oval, then the largest show ring in the world, was dedicated by Miss Dorothy James, daughter of Governor Arthur H. James. Commemorating the twentieth anniversary of the incorporation of the Devon Horse Show and Country Fair, a bronze tablet bearing the names of the

founders was unveiled: Dr. Thomas Ashton, Mrs. Archibald Barklie and William H. Wanamaker, Jr., for whom the Oval was named. The new ring was so constructed and drained that "poor footing would never again be a problem at Devon." It was a good try.

Interlude: The War Years

The number of classes at Devon swelled to 244 in 1941, then dropped back to 211 in 1942, the last time the show was held during the war years. The public letters from retired cavalry colonels continued, emphasizing the importance to the war effort of horse breeding, showing and racing. In justice to the colonels who, like Field Marshall Haig, never gave up no matter how many men they lost, it should be pointed out that the Russians fielded 54 *divisions* of horse cavalry on the Eastern front during World War II; that the last successful cavalry charge in history took place in 1942—Italian cavalry *vs.* Russian infantry before Stalingrad; and that John Burkholder, a major who was later to serve as Devon's manager, would find himself running a U.S. Army remount depot in Italy. Alas, it supplied mostly mules for mountain transport.

Horse shows in general found themselves in difficult straits from 1942 until 1945. Many of them simply dropped out of sight. Others, like Devon, retained their standing by continuing to reserve their customary dates with the AHSA, without holding an exhibit. The AHSA itself, many of whose officers and directors were associated with Devon, drastically reduced its activities. During one year of the war, it operated on a total budget of $5000. The ladies of the Country Fair devoted themselves to war work.

But the show world was only dormant. Devon revived with a start in 1946 with the

(Above) *The 'Big Three' at Devon in 1952: (l to r) William H. Ashton, William C. Hunneman, Jr., and Ward Sullivan.*

(Below, right) *Frank Ellis. As treasurer of Devon he put the show on a solid footing after a decline in the 1950's.*

fiftieth anniversary show. Mr. Beale continued as honorary president with Charlton Yarnall as president; William H. Wanamaker, Jr. and Isaac H. Clothier, Jr. served as vice presidents.

Clothier, who died in 1961 at the age of eighty-five, is a good example of the moving spirit of Devon. Although a director for most of his life—the only lifetime director the show has appointed—he hardly ever served in an executive capacity. He first showed in 1918 and was active thereafter as an enthusiastic exhibitor. He continued financial support and served as the ambassador from Devon at other major shows in the United States and abroad.

William C. Hunneman, Jr., one of Devon's most active presidents, is credited with the revival of Devon after its wartime dormancy, and with the institution of nighttime classes.

23

The Democratization of Devon

In the early 1950s, it became apparent to many that something was wrong. While the Country Fair continued to turn in ever-increasing amounts to the Bryn Mawr Hospital, attendance at the Horse Show was down. Worse, the number of exhibitors began to fall drastically. One year, only 300 exhibitors sent in advance registrations until a telephone campaign brought the number up to an acceptable level.

Various reasons for the decline were debated in committee. There was the general depressing effect of the Cold War and the Korean War, but the economy was booming and horse shows proliferated in areas of the country that had never seen them before. California, in particular, was building spectacular facilities with contributions from horse-racing revenue. The number of horses in the United States, far from diminishing in the unequal contest with the automobile, was actually increasing rapidly. Before World War I, *Rider and Driver* had estimated that $250,000 was invested in hunters and saddle horses in the countryside around Devon. In 1953, that figure could have been multiplied ten times.

The lack of exhibitors was due to something that no one cared to bring up in committee—the same thing that had killed the old Bryn Mawr Horse Show which had finally given up the ghost after World War II—an impression among exhibitors, whether right or wrong, that only members of a clique could be in the ribbons consistently.

The large estates around Devon continued faithful, but their contribution could no longer assure a successful show. Other show circuits, in the South, the Midwest and the West, were becoming equally prestigious and exhibitors had a choice of good shows. In short, Devon was no longer the only game in town.

Even those exhibitors who trusted the judging—in fairness, the list of judges always remained above reproach—were put off by a certain amount of Old Philadelphia snobbery left over from the twenties. This exclusivity made them feel left out, even if they had the best horses in the ring.

This type of elitism affected multimillionaire exhibitors and it left the general public completely cold. They came to see the horses. But the attitude of exclusivity affected even general attendance. If exhibitors did not bring horses, then no spectators would come to see them. Also, Devon had never made concessions to popular appeal. In the accounts of the twenties and thirties, it was a pride of the show that nothing, no special events, no Country Fair midway, was allowed to detract from the purity of the exhibitions. Finally, the press which lavished attention on every other sporting event in Philadelphia ran items about Devon on the society page. (It is only in recent years that Devon coverage has become sports coverage.)

To survive, Devon would have to change. As usual in times of crisis, the show had the right people to make it happen. Mr. and Mrs. Charles L. Harper were delegated to make *all* exhibitors welcome at parties and in a hospitality tent replete with bountiful infusions of charm and bourbon. The Harpers have performed with distinction for the past thirty years. Lawrence Kelley and other show officials became unofficial goodwill ambassadors, visiting other shows and organizations of horsemen in the South and Midwest to let people know that things had

After its revival in 1966, the Carriage Marathon rapidly became one of the most popular events at Devon.

Open jumper champion Idle Dice, Rodney Jenkins up, at the top of his form in 1971.

changed, that they would be among friends and treated fairly. The general public, through the newspapers, radio and television was innundated with publicity and a wide range of popular attractions, some of which were successful and some not. To president Thomas F. Bright, an advertising executive, must be given the credit for making Devon a major spectator event. James K. Robinson, Jr. was instrumental in reinstituting the driving classes, with the result that Devon is the only show in the country with regular competition in this popular event.

The Western classes also date from this period. They were a popular and controversial feature of the show until just a few years ago. The committee started small, with a few classes for Arabians (not strictly Western at all), then—getting into the swing of things—added Western pleasure classes, parade horses, quarter horses, cutting horses and, finally, demonstrations of barrel racing and bareback jumping.

The Western classes proved to be great crowd pleasers, especially the cutting horses. New to most Easterners, they were prominently covered by television and in motion pictures especially made to publicize the show. In the Devon style, good judges were appointed and the events attracted the best horses—horses that combined the ability to turn on a dime with what can only be described as extrasensory perception, an instinctive advance knowledge of exactly what a steer was going to try next. The fineness and ability of these horses was an education to many Eastern horsemen, as well as a shot in the arm to Devon attendance. Unfortunately, the cutting horses also cut up the turf too much and the events were reluctantly dropped.

In the old days at Devon, one of the most exciting classes was for runabouts. Held out-side the ring, the class was judged on speed as well as form, and sometimes amounted to a trotting race in the best New England country fair style. One of the new attractions in the Wanamaker Oval captured something of the same interest—a chariot race, first held in 1958. Little Roman chariots, devised by Iowa congressman Bill Winkelman, were drawn by teams of four Shetland ponies and competed as demonstrations. Since there is no dearth of driving skill among officials and exhibitors at Devon, the races were hotly contested. If there had been Ben-Hur-like knives on the axle hubs, the competitors would have used them.

With the advent of publicity came the celebrities, often sponsored by the radio or television station that covered the show. In the year of the chariot race, Robinson carried Gypsy Rose Lee into the ring—the Devon mud was deep and Gypsy was going to present a trophy.

Arthur Godfrey showed up often as an exhibitor and with his dressage horse Goldie. Hopalong Cassidy was there, with the entire roster of old-time television from Chief Halftown to Sally Starr, plus Mr. Rivets, Dick Clark, Chuck Wagon Pete, Tab Hunter, Jonny Rivers' jumping Brahma Bull, Amigo, and Buster the Chimp. General Eisenhower came out from Gettysburg. In later days, Jack Klugman of "The Odd Couple" was host to a successful outing of the Big Brothers, Howard Cosell presented a trophy, and such notables as Engelbert Humperdinck and Paul Williams have put in appearances.

Frank H. Ellis, III took charge of the grounds, then in disrepair, and built them up again just as the show was regaining its prosperity. He is responsible for the most recent building boom at Devon, including what is now the exhibitors' grandstand, the information

27

booth and other structures at the entrance to the grounds, and "Ellis Island," the press box, offices and committee stand at the northern end of the ring, built in 1965. Ellis had the gift of extracting money for improvements from every imaginable source, including the Country Fair, and what he could not raise he contributed himself. He is also said to have been very handy with a hammer and at driving a water wagon to wet down the ring. His death in 1966 was a severe blow to Devon, but he had helped to set it on a new and successful course.

From 1946 to his death in 1964, the show was managed by Frederick G. (Freddy) Pinch, probably among horse people the best-known personage at Devon. He rode at Devon for the first time in 1912. As manager of Dilwyne Stables, he trained some of the best hunters ever shown at Devon.

In later life he retired to his own residence, Shell Bark Farm, and was much in demand as a judge at horse shows in the United States and Canada. John Burkholder, the show's current manager, worked with Pinch in the early sixties.

In 1961, *Sports Illustrated* carried an item by Alice Higgins about a new type of contest that would do much to increase horse show attendance throughout the United States, Devon included: "In the special FEI class (which was televised in the New York and Philadelphia areas) William Robertson, a twenty-year-old amateur making his debut in open jumping, rode his thoroughbred Le Bon Chat, to victory after two jump-offs." She chats a bit more about Robertson, who had received coaching from Olympic rider George Morris (another Devon regular) and went on to give the results of the other jumping classes. But from that first exhibition, FEI classes have come to be the major spectator attraction at Devon and at all other big shows. FEI classes rapidly edged out the AHSA Table I

28

events, which had a more complex system of scoring based on points for front and hind leg touches, as well as for refusals and knockdowns. FEI classes were easy to understand, spectacular and, best of all, brought back the thrill of jumping against the clock that had been lost when "speed" classes for hunters over the outside course were dropped.

In 1966 the Carriage Marathon, now one of the show's most popular features, was begun to replace the former Coaching Marathon (*q.v.*) which had been cancelled for several years because of lack of four-in-hand entries. The Carriage Marathon, in a further demonstration of the new democracy, was open to all horsedrawn vehicles.

Due to a continuing educational program by president Tom Bright and publicity chairman Bill Bryan—author of *The Horse with the Flying Tail*—audiences were becoming more sophisticated and more interested in equestrian events for themselves. The celebrities and demonstrations necessary for survival early in the decade tapered off, while attendance continued to increase. More and more exhibitors, attracted by Devon's hospitality, good judging and efficient management, returned each year. The show was definitely over the hump.

Two major changes took place in 1969. A new grandstand was added just to the south of the main grandstand built in 1923. The old outside course was finally laid to rest, to be replaced by what is now the Gold Ring.

The grandstand, because of increased attendance and the demand and waiting list for boxes, had become a necessity. It also provided a permanent clubhouse under the stands for entertaining exhibitors and visitors, replacing the old hospitality tent.

The outside course was also a victim of popularity. People had a habit of walking across it while hunter classes were in progress, even in the early days. Celeste McNeal

*Devon's children's weekend climaxes with the family class, won in 1971 by the
Henry Hulick Family.*

One of Devon's most famous hunters, the chestnut gelding Iron Man retires the Corinthian Cup, having won it three times.

Harper recalls jumping a "triple" in one class—rail fence, baby carriage, rail fence. With bigger crowds, avoiding pedestrians finally became a regular hazard and the course was dismantled over the protests of the traditionalists, who thought that it should be fenced instead. The new Gold Ring, however, was larger than the former second ring, and the area that had been occupied by the old oval became a schooling area, so people could continue to be run down if they so desired.

In 1965, there occurred an event that left no doubt, if any had existed, that Devon had entered the twentieth century—what later became known as the exhibitors' revolt. The demonstration had many causes, but the primary one was that sixties cliché, lack of communication: in this case between management and exhibitors. Shows had multiplied and the sport had grown tremendously throughout the United States, but management was still geared to the days when horse showing was a family affair and problems could be ironed out by a chat with a friend.

The AHSA, at its annual meeting that year, had passed new rules designed to increase safety, standardize apparel and prevent cruelty in training. Devon was the first show after the meeting and the new rules had just been published. Management, however, felt constrained to enforce the current regulations; exhibitors were sent out of the ring for improper attire or identification. A horse being poled with an iron bar was reported. (Poleing is tapping a horse around the pasterns with a stick, usually a bamboo pole, as it jumps a fence to make it pick up its feet higher. It was much used before jumping classes where touches counted.)

The poleing incident was the last straw. Exhibitors felt insulted and injured by the strict enforcement of rules that many of them knew nothing about. Without direct access to the show management there was little they could do about it, but some of them approached Mrs. Scott about the problem. She met with president Tom Bright and chairman James Robinson, but before any accommodation could be reached between the two factions, the USET jumping class was called.

The committee watched in amazement, if not horror, as the contestants entered the ring in a variety of odd costumes and funny hats and proceeded to jump the course backward, sidewise or any way fancy took them. In the ensuing chaos everybody had lots of fun except the judges and stewards, who risked their lives by entering the ring.

Things eventually calmed down. The riders, not all of whom had participated in the revolt, offered apologies, cooler heads prevailed and the show proceeded as usual. No one was disciplined—after all, who is to say whether a runaway is the idea of the rider or the horse?

Devon was not the only show to be affected by exhibitors' resentment of both regulations and the quality of judging; demonstrations occurred at other places for several months.

After the show, with the consent of the committee Mrs. Scott and Tom Bright asked James Fallon, manager of the National Horse Show in New York, if he could come to Devon as manager, with John Burkholder as general manager. Fallon, a director of the AHSA who has also done valuable work on a number of its most important committees, is well liked by exhibitors. In addition to his other duties at the show, he serves as a sort of ombudsman for exhibitors' rights. His work during the show and advice about the selection of judges have improved management-exhibitor relations and helped to make

Devon a happy show for the past decade.

The seventy-fifth anniversary show was held in 1971, with appropriate ceremonies. The program contained a letter from Mrs. Helen Warren Holladay of Rapidan, Virginia, the only living person who had exhibited at Devon in 1896, and included a history of Devon by its historian, Raymond S. Cox.

The USET Challenge Trophy that year was won by a horse named Idle Dice.

Victory over the Elements

The anniversary show also witnessed the final round in Devon's battle against the mud. Because of the ever-increasing number of entries, the traffic in the rings and schooling areas had become tremendous and the old sod was torn up within a day. A rule of thumb for pasturing horses is one acre per horse: one square foot less and you have a swamp. Now Devon had about 1200 horses on 27 acres and although they did not graze (except once in a while around the edges of the barns), they soon transformed the turf into a kind of viscous mortar. And if, by some quirk of fate, it did not rain, the clouds of dust raised from the bare earth were equally hard on exhibitors and horses alike. Mrs. Scott and her co-chairman of the grounds committee, Mrs. Lewis, were, like their predecessors, deluged with pleas for help.

At the suggestion of Jim Fallon, they called in the dean of racetrack builders, Richard Strickland, who is responsible for the courses at Belmont, Aqueduct and Saratoga. He said they were asking what was very nearly impossible, since Devon needed a hard track for harness horses; a softer footing for hunters and jumpers; other footings for other divisions. He decided to give it a try anyway, warning that the ground would

take two years to settle properly. The committee raised the substantial amount of money required, including some very generous individual donations, and work began.

Devon Director Syl Quigley's construction firm excavated the rings and schooling areas to the drains, extended the drainage system and filled the area with 8 inches of modified screenings (a mixture of limestone and cement that remains porous without shifting position like gravel). The base was then covered with 3 inches of loamy sand (90 percent sand and 10 percent loam) for good footing. The ring slopes 19 inches from side to side, down toward the drains. Imperceptible to the eye, the slope is nevertheless enough to drain off most of the water.

For the first two years, everyone was miserable except the jumpers, who had the best footing ever. The wheels of wagons and carriages sank halfway to their hubs in the sand and Mrs. Scott became very unpopular. But the third year proved Strickland right. While still a little deep for heavy carriages, the ring has become known for the best footing in the United States. Both the ring and the schooling area foundations are being copied by many shows.

The dust problem has been solved by three annual applications of a new soil settling compound. Riders and drivers both appreciate the sure footing, and those who present trophies no longer have to take off their shoes or don hip boots to enter the ring, in spite of some of the wettest shows on record in recent years.

In 1975, using donations from exhibitors and friends, a new twenty-stall barn was built just behind the east grandstand. The added space convenient to the ring helped make it possible to reinstate the Hackney horse classes; otherwise the exhibitors

32

A large pony hunter champion, Take A Bow, is a study in elegance.

The most famous American saddlebred shown at Devon, Dodge Stables' Wing Commander, sired generations of champions.

Wing Commander in later years. (Photographs of Wing Commander courtesy of "Saddle and Bridle".)

Sensation Rex, leading American saddlebred sire, photographed in 1938.

would have had to drive their vehicles through traffic to reach the ring. Few full-size Hackneys are now being bred in the United States and Canada, although Hackney ponies remain popular. Devon is one of the few shows that still have Hackney classes and it is hoped that they can be continued: encouragement of Hackney breeding was one of Devon's original purposes and the Hackney remains its emblem.

Another major change in 1975 was the elimination of the first-year green working hunter classes. There is no way to qualify first-year green working hunters, since the class is for horses that are in their first year of showing, and entries generally totaled between eighty and a hundred. Stabling for this number of entries and the time consumed in judging the classes finally became too much of a burden, as the number of horses swelled in other divisions. There was little protest about cancellation of the class; even the owners seemed to have realized that it was too much of a good thing. Second-year green working hunters, where the committee can exercise its judgment in qualifying entries, remain in contention.

Filling in for the green hunters were the reinstated Hackney classes and new events for amateur owner-jumpers. In some ways these new classes, typifying Devon's traditional devotion to a place for the amateur, were even more exciting than the open jumper classes. In the crude sense there were more wrecks; but for those who knew something about the sport, there was an added excitement in the wider variation of methods and abilities of both horse and rider, a greater degree of chance in the outcome, and a more open sense of competition. There was also more identification of the spectators with the contestants. Standing around the ring were many riders who might have been

thinking, "I could be in there myself." The winners had the satisfaction of knowing that they and the horses had done it singlehandedly. Finally, everybody had fun—as if they had been at a country hunter trial instead of a sports spectacular which, in the last analysis, is what Devon is all about.

Devon stepped outside the bounds of all tradition in 1975 by holding the show on *Sunday* for the first time in its history. Only in the afternoon, of course, so it wouldn't detract from churchgoing, but there *was* a competition (an open jumper stake) in addition to an exhibit of dressage and the Carriage Marathon, which is more a display than a contest. Only those who remember not being able to attend a movie or play cards on a rainy Sunday afternoon are capable of appreciating the change in attitudes that a Sunday meeting represents. So far no church groups have demonstrated and the committee has not even received a letter of protest. It is true that the best day for the largest number of people to see the Marathon is Sunday, but the founding fathers must be turning over in their graves.

Since 1919, The Devon Horse Show and Country Fair has been a gigantic corporation. Correct in a business sense, the word is even more proper in its original meaning: Devon is a *body*, a living organism which has been able to survive by changing and adapting. It dies off in one area and puts out shoots in another, but the oak tree remains recognizably an oak.

There is no question that Devon will survive and grow, within the limitations imposed by time—a week down in Devon is now nine days—and the size of the grounds, now hemmed in by suburbia. The tremendous growth of interest in horses and horse sports since the war and Devon's reputation as a testing ground for champions in other shows make its recurrence as certain as anything can be in our times.

The question for those who love it is whether its character can survive financial pressures, the temptations of professional sports, and the tendency to commercialize any event that attracts large numbers of people.

I think, perhaps optimistically, that it can. There is a continuity at Devon, in the long association of certain families with it and in its custom of bringing its officers up through the ranks, that provides a hard core of resistance. Every development that takes place at Devon must withstand the test of this resistance; while the winds of change may break off a few branches, the tree refuses to bend. Devon is a singularly sturdy way of life. But then, horse people are in touch with a deeper reality than most of us.

This theory can be tested still in a number of places: on junior days, when the new generation of riders shows the same enthusiasm (and despair) that its great-grandfathers did in 1896; in barns on rainy nights when horse people talk about the same things, make the same deals and play the same games as they did in Surtees' or Dickens' time; in the show office, where the same harassed officials confront the same frantic exhibitors; in the Country Fair, where the granddaughter of a founder may be slapping a hot dog in a roll; or best of all, on a sunny weekday morning when, with only the devotees to watch, the long streams of gleaming hunters roll over fence after fence with the hypnotic effect of a river, outside of time.

Now that we know a little of what's behind it, let's see what's happening now.

Photo by Weintraub
1116 Chestnut St. Phila. Pa.

Memorial Day, 1936. Devon was rising out of the Depression.

A Junior exhibitor in 1953 got to ride with Hopalong Cassidy.

2

Devon's Junior Weekend

Devon does not begin with a flourish of trumpets—unless you count ringmaster Honey Craven's calls on a coaching horn—nor with the raising of a curtain. On Friday morning, after endless preparation, it just seems to materialize. Suddenly there are ponies being judged in the Wanamaker Oval, while in the Gold Ring a crew sets up jumps for a class. The time schedule says 8:00 A.M., "Class 81, Welsh yearlings, colts or fillies." Spectators so far are few; most people are getting ready to exhibit their own entries. Those who have come this early in the morning to watch are free to wander.

To many, this is the best time at Devon, with the early sun on a world of horses, each intent on his own business, playing to no audience but the judges. (It's good even in the rain.) Later the crowds begin to swell, the sun gets hotter—or the wind blows colder; you can never tell at Devon—and things become more tightly organized, but for the moment everything belongs to the horses and their people.

A Tradition for the Young

Their people, except for the handlers of the pony breeding classes, are all under eighteen years old. For this is Devon's Junior Weekend, outgrowth of an eighty-year tradition of events for the young. It is one of the largest shows in the world exclusively for children, from three-year-olds in the lead line classes to fiercely competitive teenagers hoping for a spot on the U.S. Equestrian Team.

Appropriately enough, for the entire morning the Wanamaker Oval is devoted to every child's dream, the Welsh ponies. This fast-growing breed—more than 20,000 are now registered—stems originally from the sturdy mountain ponies of Wales. About 1825, a thoroughbred stallion was turned out

41

with a drove of Welsh mares. The resulting cross has many Arabian characteristics: the slightly "dished" (concave) profile, the arched neck and the high-set tail. They are solid in color, mostly gray, white or chestnut, stand less than 12.2 hands, are easy to keep and make great children's hunters because of their surefootedness and jumping ability. They seem more like good small saddle horses than the more popular Shetland.

Nearby Liseter Hall Farm, in Newtown Square, Pennsylvania, is one of the country's leading breeders of Welsh ponies, and the classes at Devon are generally dominated by Liseter-owned or bred entries. On and on they go, Welsh yearlings, Welsh two-year-old colts, Welsh two-year-old fillies, Welsh brood mares, Welsh stallions, Welsh produce of dam, Welsh get of sire, Welsh pleasure, Welsh hunter ponies, and Welsh working hunter ponies—sixteen events in all. At the end Liseter Brilliant Dream is the champion Welsh pony mare, and Rain Beau, Mr. and Mrs. Kenneth Taylor, Hampton, Virginia, champion Welsh pony stallion. And Broadaxe Be Geepers, Susan Slacum, Cockeysville, Maryland, wins the Welsh pleasure ponies championship stake and the Welsh pleasure model ponies. (She will also take a blue in a pony hunter class.)

Fans on Friday morning have their choice: the subtle pleasure of breeding classes in one ring or the more athletic excitement of junior jumpers in the other.

In the latter, the rider to watch is Robin Ann Rost, seventeen, of Branchville, New Jersey, an intent but cheerful blonde girl with a stylish way of riding that recalls the young Billy Steinkraus. Less wiry than some past female champions, such as Kathy Kusner, she looks, with her eminently correct position, as if she and the horse were inseparable.

Among the early arrivals at Devon on

Pigtails and ponies go together at Devon's Junior weekend. Shyness vanishes in the ring.

Hackney pony must learn to pose.

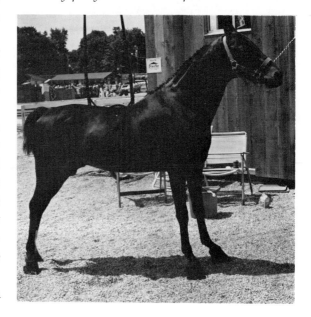

42

Both horse and rider are well groomed for a Devon lead-line class.

"You mean that's the course?"

If you're too small for a hunting cap, a safety helmet can be just as chic.

Wednesday were Robin, her mother and father, Dr. and Mrs. Robert C. Rost, two girlfriends who would help with the hard work of cleaning and show grooming, and three horses: Wigg's Bar, a fourteen-year-old chestnut gelding; Speechmaker, an aged brown gelding; and Paper Moon, an eight-year-old chestnut gelding. There is nothing unusual about bringing a string of three or even more horses to Devon's Junior Weekend, but two of Robin's, Wigg's Bar and Speechmaker, were quarter horses in a world generally reserved for thoroughbreds. Wigg's Bar won the junior jumper championship in 1972 and 1973 and Speechmaker, the junior handy hunter trophy in 1971.

Robin comes by her success with quarter horses naturally. Her mother, Joan L. Rost, exhibited in Western classes, and was her daughter's first and only trainer until 1973. At the age of seven, Robin showed her first horse at Devon, her grandfather's stallion, in a Western pleasure class. Her father, a veterinarian, has designed courses for both Devon and the National, and has managed shows in New Jersey and Massachusetts.

In her last year of showing as a junior, Robin had been winning consistently on the Florida circuit and had won the AHSA Hunter Seat Medal finals at Harrisburg in 1974 (which made her ineligible for this class

at Devon). At Devon, however, she would be competing against seventy of the country's top junior riders in ten events in the space of two days, including gigantic junior hunter and jumper classes, some with as many as forty-nine horses in a single division. Junior Weekend at Devon has become a major horse show in itself in terms of number of classes, entries and attendance.

In her first class in the Gold Ring, Paper Moon took second in the jump-off to Mrs. William Hewitt's Dirty Harry, ridden by her son Alexander. Wigg's Bar, however, was warming up in the same class, taking a sixth, and that evening he won the junior jumper fault and out for the fourth consecutive time. (A fault and out class is judged on points for as many obstacles as can be jumped in a fixed time, two points for each jumped clean and one point for a knock-down.)

In the Wanamaker Oval, Robin rode Speechmaker in the small junior hunter division, with a second to Mrs. Edie Spruance's Be My Valentine, ridden by Anne Spruance, in the first class, a fourth in the handy hunter class, and a win in the conformation class, to take the championship of the small junior hunter division and reserve grand hunter championship. The champion was Derby Hill's Isle of Erin, winner of the large hunter division, ridden by Leslie Brown, a younger

Suzanne Meyle's Hail 'n Hardy shows good form over the brush in a pony working hunter class.

Blue armbands identify competitors in the "Maclay" horsemanship event of the A.S.P.C.A.

Junior jumpers already have adult style and eagerness.

Cindy Brink on Hi Brass clears a fence with room to spare.

sister of the Buddy Brown who was to give Rodney Jenkins some stiff competition in the later open jumping events.

On Saturday morning, Robin's first ride was in the ASPCA horsemanship class, the Maclay Medal. She won it on a borrowed horse, Barn Owl.

In the next class, "junior jumpers, time first jump off," Robin had entered both Wigg's Bar and Paper Moon. For the first and only time during the show she was out of the ribbons on both. George D'Ambrosio, brother of top rider Tony D'Ambrosio, won the blue with High Priest and second with Habibi.

Both Paper Moon and Wigg's Bar were soon to have their revenge, however. They placed one and two in the modified Olympic junior jumper stake Saturday night—the third time Robin had won the trophy. This

win gave her two horses tied for the junior jumper championship.

In two days at Devon, Robin Rost had won three championships—in hunter, jumper and equitation classes—and one reserve, and had been named Best Child Rider for the second consecutive year. It was one of the best performances ever during Junior Weekend, and practically incredible considering the extent and quality of the competition.

Placing third to Robin in the Maclay was another young rider on the way up, Debra Baldi, fifteen, of Newtown. She was at Devon with her Arc Royal in the junior large hunter classes, and also rode Gerald Goldman's Dresden in the pony hunter classes. A student of George Morris, whose pupils make up a good percentage of Junior Weekend competitors, she has been riding since the age of

47

five. Arc Royal placed fifth in one junior hunter class and sixth in the handy hunters; she was second to Fredi Wells in the AHSA hunter seat medal class, and Dresden took a second in the model pony hunter (13–14.2) class. Debra was fourth in the awards for best child rider, behind Robin, Anne Spruance of Jamison, and Lindsey Anne Evans of Baltimore. As Debra said, "Receiving a third or fourth place ribbon at Devon is better than winning first at a small show, because you know the judges are tops, the class is very large, the competition is tough and the round must be extra good. Of course, those riders in equitation classes—the Medal or Maclay finals—find it the most exciting part of their years as a rider."

She should know. She showed at thirty-three shows in 1975 and was champion or reserve in junior hunter, pony or equitation classes at twenty-seven of them, from Virginia to Connecticut.

While the junior hunters are performing in the Wanamaker Oval, the pony hunters, any breed, have possession of the Gold Ring for the afternoon. Both the class size and the crowds are gigantic. There is not one of the six events that has less than forty entries, and several must be divided into two sections. The pony hunter trophies, named for previous champions, are a delight in themselves: the Squeaky Challenge Trophy, the Second Rosemary Challenge Trophy, the Midget Challenge Trophy, the Highfield's Tulip Challenge Trophy and The Third Tippety Witchet Trophy. There are model classes, under saddle classes and classes over small (2 foot, 6 inches and 3 foot) jumps. When it is finally over, the judges are exhausted. The most difficult task for a judge is a large class with only a hairsbreadth of difference between the top six contenders; they will have

48

the same thing to face again tomorrow.

After a break for dinner, shortened by the length of the afternoon classes, the events continue under the lights. The junior jumpers' fault and out is first, followed by an exhibition of mounted drill by the Valley Forge Military Academy. The musical ride by the colorfully uniformed cadets, to the accompaniment of the Academy band, has been a tradition at Devon since the 1930s. Because of the scarcity of stabling, their horses are picketed on ropes at the side of the schooling area, giving the grounds the look of a cavalry encampment.

Two large classes for junior hunters conclude the evening.

Saturday begins with the large and important ASPCA Maclay event, followed by junior jumpers, time first jump-off. The sun is out, and it is beginning to get hot even this early in the morning. The ranks are deep around the Wanamaker Oval and some gravitate to the Gold Ring, where they can sit on tree-shaded stands and watch the crossbred ponies parade. Although people who know Shetlands might dispute it, the crossbreds are simply ponies of no recognized breed, rather than those bred for bad dispositions. In spite of mixed ancestry (both sire and dam may be registered, but of different breeds), the crossbreds are attractive, high-quality stock—even the weanlings, which are a favorite with children. One peculiarity is that about half the entries are unnamed or named for sire or dam: Produce of Winamit, Tanrackin Farm, won one class, and Get of Chantain, from the same farm, won the next. An unnamed filly from Tanrackin won the crossbred pony filly or mare championship and Brighton Pen Light, Frank H. Owens, Jr., Nokesville, Virginia won the colt or stallion championship.

Empathy. Did this silent communication take place before or after the event?

A Devon Specialty

Those watching the equine youngsters in the Gold Ring were missing a Devon specialty up by the committee stand: the lead line classes, the only events at Devon where everybody wins. The first class is for children who have not reached their fourth birthday. The ponies, though shown in full tack, are guided around the ring by parents, brothers or sisters holding a lead line. The entries are judged on manners and suitability of pony to rider. Although appointments do not count, the children are usually dressed for the hunting field, complete with hunting cap, coat, vest, breeches, and either tops or jodphur boots. In the next class, for children four to six, the rules are the same, but the entries are also asked to trot their ponies. Blythe K. Gillmer of Sellersville won the under-four trophy and Sophia A. Miller of Unionville, the older division. But all fifteen in each class got a ribbon and a giant lollipop from Richard E. McDevitt, president of Devon, and James K. Robinson, Jr., chairman.

During the lunch break and the first two afternoon classes for junior hunters, the grounds began to fill up with girls in sloganed tee shirts and blue jeans. In the hospitality room under the south grandstand, the reason for the sudden influx—singer Paul Williams in mod attire and Prince Valiant haircut—was just finishing his own lunch. After the experience in 1974 with Engelbert Humperdinck, it seemed advisable to convey Williams to the ring by car, rather than battle through the throng. His car sneaked in through a back gate, he bolted into it pursued by a couple of sharp teenagers, and proceeded by a circuitous route to the committee stand, while his entourage and the other celebrities of WIP Day at

50

In the older (ages four-to-six) lead-line class, most of the riders seem ready for the hunt.

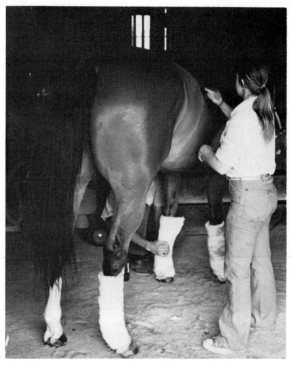

Good preparation in the stable is half the battle.

A canter on the longe line both trains and exercises. Practices of dressage are being used more and more in hunter and jumper training.

Devon made their way on foot as best they could. Philadelphia's station WIP—and before it, WPVI—has brought various stars to Devon each year on the first Saturday of the show to help increase attendance, especially at the Country Fair where they sign autographs after introductions and a short song or monologue in the ring.

The weather had changed. It was still very hot, but a strong wind had come up, and although Ken Garland struggled valiantly with the microphone, the speeches were difficult to hear through the static and rumble. No matter, Paul Williams was *there* and so were his fans, and that was enough for them. In the meantime, John Burkholder wanted to keep to his schedule and the junior hunter stake (under 16.0) began.

The pony hunter classes, going on simultaneously in the Gold Ring, were similar to Friday's in size and quality. When they

were over, Brett Kligerman on his gray gelding Westwood Dinadan had won the A section of the small pony division and the grand pony championship, with 15 points. The B section champion was Lynn De Roetth's Orion; Southern Gray, Shelly Guyer up, won the large pony championship for the second consecutive year. In the AHSA Medal, Fredi Welles won his fourth victory, qualifying him for the championship finals at Harrisburg in the fall.

A Family Affair

The last events of Junior Weekend in the Gold Ring are pony hunt teams, and the parent and child class. In the first, won by a team of Rachael Baker, Louise Lefferts and Ellen Ross, a team of ponies follow one another over a course of fences in the ring, keeping a safe hunting distance. They are judged on per-

51

Last minute touches and advice before a saddle seat equitation class.

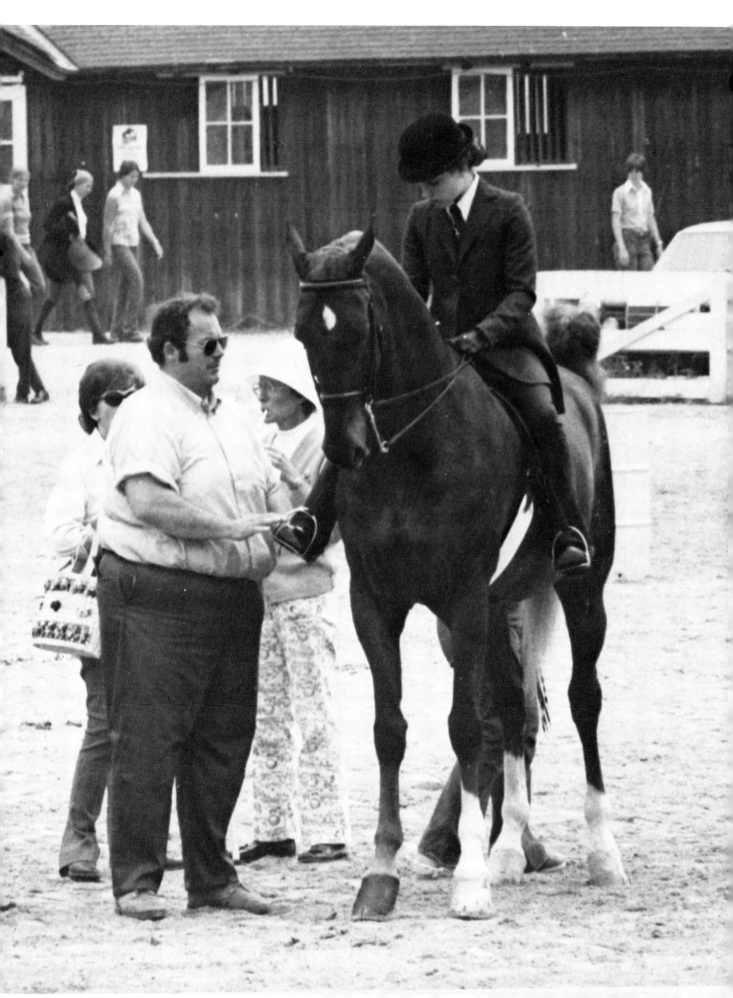

formance, suitability, manners and appearance as a team. In the parent and child class for the Rose Tree Cup, the same type of hunting course, with jumps about 3 feet in height, is ridden by a team consisting of a parent and child. It is judged 75 percent on performance and 25 percent on suitability of mounts to riders. This class was won by the winner of the large pony championship, Shelly Guyer, and her mother, Mrs. David L. Guyer.

The last classes of the evening session were also a family affair: the horse hunt teams and the family class. The horse hunt teams are a last vestige of the days when Devon was actually a hunter trial for the surrounding clubs, and teams from Rose Tree, Radnor and the rest competed among themselves in a wide variety of team classes, including one where four members had to jump six fences abreast. The hunt teams now are mostly made up from scratch (post entries are allowed) and the last time a hunt club entry won was when Radnor took the class in 1970. The 1975 winners were Debbie Thorington, Malvern, and Fran Benson and Beth Benson, Pineville. The fourth-place team was composed of riders from Connecticut, New York and Pennsylvania.

Any child exhibiting at Devon has had parental support and understanding far beyond the call of duty. It was thus entirely fitting that Junior Weekend should end on Saturday night with a family class (any set of relations, but usually father, mother and child), riding three horses at a sedate walk, trot and center, judged on manners and suitability. In 1975 the event was won by the Raffensperger family, Ft. Washington, and second place went to the Heath family of Wilmington, who had won in 1973 and 1974. The Browns, the Guyers, the Sheldrakes and the Inmans also placed, but the committee might have awarded a ribbon to every parent

who has cleaned stalls, groomed horses, driven vans overnight, soothed hurt feelings or merely stood around during the interminable delays of a show. The ribbon would be lettered "invaluable service to the cause of horsemanship in the United States" in dollar-bill green with a Turquoise (protector against falls) in the center.

How serious is the Junior Weekend at Devon? From mere observation, it is hard to say. Most of the competitors seem to enjoy themselves, meet friends, and stay up late talking in barns. By the time they reach Devon, most of them are too experienced to cry over being shut out of the ribbons (a common occurrence in smaller shows). Most of the parents realize that protesting the judges' decision is futile, but the competitiveness is still there. Devon is a testing ground for entry into many phases of the horse world, from the Olympics to a post as a trainer or instructor.

Taken all in all, to one who decries intense competition in any kind of children's sports, riding is relatively gentle compared to, for instance, Little League baseball. The children do it mainly because they like it, not from parental or group pressure; they compete in the ring but not outside it. Riding, being exactly the opposite of a big-money sport, is not the ticket to a million-dollar contract.

Another aspect of equestrian sports for children that is worthy of especial note: they are the only sports where boys and girls, or men and women, can compete on an equal basis.

Junior Weekend at Devon is the fastest-growing part of the show, even with the type of stringent qualifications exemplified by Debra Baldi's 1975 record. The implications of this for the future of the show are encouraging.

Two ways of standing. (Above) Judging for conformation in a pony roadster class (below), *at attention in a conformation hunter event.*

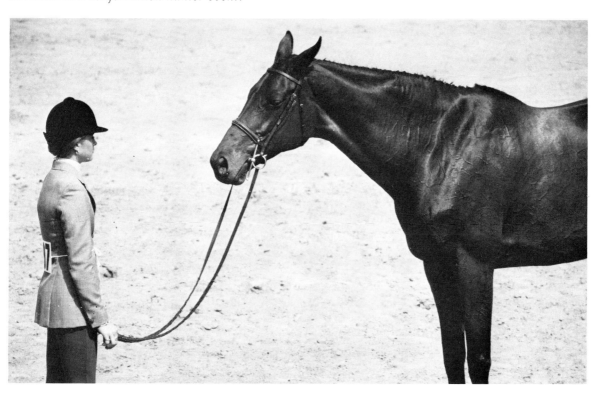

The Carriage Marathon

Sunday morning at Devon 1975, following Junior Weekend, was even more chaotic than usual. The exhibitors in the senior division, who ordinarily have all day to move into the stalls vacated by the juniors, were pressed to finish by 12:30, when the gates would be opened to the public and van traffic would stop. Most of them were anxious to be under cover anyway, since the heat of Saturday had been replaced overnight by rain and unseasonable cold. At least the barn and tents, heated by 1200 horses, would be warm and dry.

From 12:30 until the entry of the first vehicle in the Carriage Marathon, there was not much for anyone to do without a horse to look after. The booths selling food at the Country Fair were open, but not many of the other shops, due to Pennsylvania's blue laws. Miss Elizabeth Lewis, of Marietta, Georgia, saved the day with a classic exhibition of dressage. Mounted on her dark brown Trakehner, on an improvised rectangular manege marked by flower pots, Miss Lewis demonstrated an intricate series of voltes, two tracks, shoulder-ins, turns on the forehand, piaffes and the other airs of high school dressage, all to a quiet rarely heard around the show ring. After an encore, she received a large bouquet of roses from the show committee.

Dressage, a system of training movements in which the horse's gaits are shortened and raised by bringing the balance rearward to lighten the forehand and promote a special type of agility, is becoming increasingly popular in the United States. A dressage show held on the Devon grounds some months afterward was the most successful in years.

57

Mrs. J. Austin Du Pont drives her own team of matched Welsh ponies in the Devon Carriage Marathon.

Thousands of spectators, enticed by the first Sunday showing at Devon in its history, sat huddled in raincoats around the Wanamaker Oval sipping cups of coffee, the hottest-selling item at the Country Fair, or jogging in place to keep their wet feet from freezing. A ripple spread through the crowd—"They're coming"—and into the ring rolled a pony cart containing three lovely girls in yellow summer dresses that would have been appropriate for Scarlet O'Hara at a garden party. They were followed by a procession of ladies and gentlemen in horsedrawn vehicles of every description, eighty-eight in all, alike only in their disregard of climatic conditions. Some of the ladies carried fringed parasols. It was the end of May and, by God, they were dressed for the season and there was nothing that a little Canadian cold front could do about it.

Devon is like that. And the participants in the Carriage Marathon, like the whips of the driving competitions, are among the staunchest upholders of Devonian unflappability. Rain, mud, cold, runaways or searing heat, it is all alike to them.

Mrs. Frank Haydon, the celebrated British whip, is an example. In 1961 the ring was so flooded that the ringmaster blew the Navy swimming call to announce the coaching class. Mrs. Haydon entered the ring driv-

ing the Brewster Park Drag of New York's Commodore Chancey Stillman, behind four matched Hackneys. The rain came down in sheets. The narrow tires of the four-in-hand coach sank over their rims in mud, the lightning crackled, and Mrs. Haydon said, "It rains in England too. Let's get on with it." And she did, guiding the Hackneys through the blue-painted barrels of the course without a tick to win the class.

Assembly at Blackburn

Fourteen years later, eighty-eight carriages had assembled early in the morning at Blackburn Farm in Berwyn to get ready for the four-and-one-half-mile run—four for ponies—to Devon. Blackburn Farm is the residence of Mrs. C. Edward Pacaud, the mother of Henry L. Collins III, a coaching enthusiast and assistant vice president of the Horse Show and Country Fair, who revived the Carriage Marathon in 1966.

There have always been coaching classes at Devon. To a great extent that was what the first show was all about, but the Carriage Marathon is something relatively new. For many years it was a *coaching* marathon, open only to park drags or road coaches drawn by teams of four.

Elizabeth Lewis executes a "pass" during an exhibition of dressage.

No dust will mar the lacquer of this authentically restored British road coach.

The current marathon is open to all horsedrawn vehicles and there is a time limit of forty minutes to cover four-and-one-half miles. After World War II, the number of coaches participating in the marathon dwindled gradually, until the event died out entirely. When Collins revived it in 1966, it was open to all vehicles and a total of sixteen entered, about ten more than had regularly participated in the coaching event. In 1967, twenty-three entries arrived. By 1972, the number had swelled to eighty-eight and it has remained between eighty and one hundred ever since, the largest assembly of horsedrawn vehicles to participate in any regular event in the United States. Nearly all of the entries are authentic period pieces lovingly restored, many of them dating from the reign of Queen Victoria and some from the

60

period before the Civil War. Only about one percent are reproductions or new carriages, usually homemade.

While coaching is usually considered a rich man's sport, with a park drag running as much as $50,000 for coach, harness and a matched team of four, the sport of driving is open to anyone with a backyard horse. A variety of authentic carts and gigs are available—according to advertisements in *The Carriage Journal,* for between $1000 and $2000. The popularity of the sport is growing rapidly, for a variety of reasons. One is probably nostalgia for a more leisurely past. The second is the opportunity to use a family pet, perhaps a pony outgrown by a child, or a horse no longer ridden but kept for sentimental reasons. There is also a certain factor of snob appeal, but most drivers simply

A tandem hitch in the Marathon gives a startled gray room to dance.

enjoy the feeling of driving—the quiet, the feeling of speed and the instant responsiveness of a well-trained horse. The thrill of driving has been compared to sailing or gliding: man, not machine, is once more in control and motion is due to the forces of nature.

"Horsedrawn vehicles" covers a lot of ground. At Blackburn that morning in 1975, there are hay wagons and phaetons, gigs and jaunting cars, ice wagons, dog carts, basket phaetons, park drags, road coaches, Amish buggies, mail vans and governess carts—drawn by one, two, three or four horses or ponies. In past marathons there have also been hansom cabs and hearses.

They assemble early to clean and polish coachwork, groom horses, gossip, picnic and parade for a preliminary judging before the run. Some camp out in the field the night

before. The judges look at the vehicles once at the farm, then at points along the route and, finally, in the ring.

In previous years, ribbons have been awarded in eight divisions, with two divisions, light commerical vehicles and farm vehicles, eligible for ribbons in their class but not for the championship. This year all participants will receive a bronze plate and a ribbon, and champion and reserve will be chosen from the entries as a whole.

In spite of the weather, there is only one mishap, a runaway. At Blackburn the entries form up in one enclosure, separated by a hedge from the field where they will circle for the judges. The Dickensian traffic jam proves too much for one pony, who decides to make for less confined quarters, gets involved with the hedge and smashes his cart into kindling.

61

Devon Chairman James K. Robinson, Jr. drives a Brewster park coach in four-in-hand driving competition.

An unusual combination of a tandem hitch with a gig.

Clement R. Hoopes, a well-known whip, shows a Hackney horse to a gig.

Many of the vehicles in the Carriage Marathon date to the Victorian era or earlier.

Luckily, neither pony nor driver is hurt. There have been no injuries in the history of the marathon. Racing or jockeying for position are cause for disqualification and drivers must be eighteen or accompanied by an adult.

The Judges, Mrs. Scott Hill, Jr. and President of the American Carriage Association, Hugh Holbrook, with the assistance of David Dallas O'Dell, Mr. and Mrs. Blackwell, and Mrs. John MacDonald have finished their cold, wet job at the farm by 3 P.M.; the run is about to begin. The assistant judges will help to spot along the route and a veterinarian is standing by to check the horses for soundness of wind and limb as they enter the ring.

For convenience this year, and or separate judging in other years, the entries have been broken down into eight categories: single horse or single pony; harness pairs, ponies or horses; unicorns, three or four-in-hands of ponies or horses; farm vehicles and light commercial vehicles. They will be judged briefly once more in the ring and the finalists asked to parade for selection of the grand champion and reserve.

A Magnificent Spectacle

And they're off. The tree-lined blacktop of Sugartown Road resounds with the regular clop-clop of hooves, the rumble of iron-tired wheels, and the squeaking of springs and axles. Forty minutes later the first carriage enters the ring.

For almost an hour the equipages enter by the east gate, circle a few times around the Wanamaker Oval and depart by the south gate. Some remain in the schooling area, waiting for the final judging, while others start the trip back to Blackburn Farm by a route three miles shorter than the Marathon course.

The crowd stays by the rail despite the

"Let me out of here. I only got a fifth and I want to go home."

64

There's ample power in this pair for an even heavier load.

How the mail was delivered in the era of the penny postcard.

weather, which has become even colder and more blustery, because there is no sameness about the marathon. Each carriage is an individual. It is hard to believe that a wheeled vehicle designed to be pulled by a horse could have developed such a multiplicity of forms, sizes and colors. There are Irish jaunting cars, gigantic two-wheelers, tiny governess carts made of wickerwork like the basket phaeton, which also makes an appearance. Some are painted, some lacquered, some varnished, but all show evidence of loving care in restoration and maintenance.

The horses, too, are all different, ranging from the smallest Shetland pony to crossbred coach horses, half Hackney and half Clydesdale. Some are pure elegance, others stocky and built low to the ground like the Shetlands, who were once used to pull mine cars in England. All seem well behaved, in spite of the wind that blows their manes and ruffles their coats the wrong way, something most

horses hate. And finally there are the drivers, all of them obviously enjoying themselves. While the marathon frowns on period dress, the appropriate costumes for driving—no matter when made—often seem anachronistic, like the carriages themselves. There is a man who looks like Abraham Lincoln, complete with beard and top hat; one who seems more like Santa Claus, with coaching horn; there are ladies in summer pastels, ladies with mohair shawls, ladies in huge picture hats, accompanied by small dogs, as if in a Goya painting, and others in severe Amish black. The spectators love it. The nineteenth century has returned for an hour.

They particularly like a wagonette driven by Susan Saltonstall of Massachusetts. A delicate green four-wheeled carriage, drawn by four matched Welsh ponies in black and silver harness, it is straight out of a fairy tale. The judges like it, too, and Miss Saltonstall is awarded the championship.

66

The Saddlebreds

Among the first events on Memorial Day, 1975, is Class 222, three-gaited novice, beginning a series of twenty-five riding and driving classes for American Saddlebreds to be held throughout the remainder of the week.

Devon is regaining the prominence in saddle horse exhibits that it had before the war, when manager Tom Clark attracted the top three-gaited, five-gaited and fine harness entries from throughout the United States.

When the Devon show began, saddle horse classes were judged by "their conformation, quality, manners and ability to carry the weight specified. They will be required to back easily, change the lead on the canter without apparent effort, and stand long enough for the rider to dismount and mount without unnecessary trouble." Although the American Saddlebred existed at the time, judges were not particular about breed affilia-

tions. Saddle horses were generally shown with docked tails.

The change in fashion to long-flowing manes and tails on five-gaited horses, the establishment of a registered breed, and the division of Saddlebreds into three-gaited (walk, trot and canter), five-gaited (walk, trot, canter, rack and slow gait) and fine harness horses, took several decades of showing. It was not until the 1930s that the classes as we know them at Devon took their current form.

The period between the wars was the peak of Saddlebred showing at Devon, with entries from as far away as California. After World War II, national entries began to decline and their places were filled primarily by local entries, although such major contenders as the Dodge Stables remained faithful, with such brilliant entries as world champion Wing Commander (1948–1954).

A night class in the Wanamaker Oval. Lights were not installed until after World War II.

Near faultless form of horse and rider in a ladies' three-gaited saddlebred class.

At suspension in the canter, an American saddlebred has all four feet off the ground.

A Good Omen

Evidence of the Saddlebred comeback at Devon is not hard to find. In 1973, the Eastern Saddle Horse Breeder's Association, founded by a group of breeders who showed primarily at Devon, honored the show by bringing the Association's three champions to Devon for presentation of their awards. The same was done in 1975. In 1974, the well-known Saddlebred trainer Tom Moore showed at Devon for the first time, with entries from Jean McLean Davis's Oak Hill Farm, Harrodsburg, Kentucky: a good omen for the future of this division. He was back again in 1975, cleaning up in five-gaited, three-gaited and fine harness classes. The competition in Saddlebred classes becomes stronger each year. The breaking of the division into a large number of sections provides an opportunity for horse and rider to compete with the best of their peers. There are limit classes for those

horses which have not won six firsts (or some other limit to entries may be set), novice classes for those which have not won three. Junior exhibitor classes (stallions prohibited) are for riders or drivers who have not reached the age of eighteen, while junior classes are for horses under four years of age. Amateur owner classes are for exhibitors who own their horses or for members of their immediate families. Open classes are open to any qualified entry, while others may be open only to horses above or below a certain height, say 15 hands, 2 inches (62 inches) at the withers, and so on. The object is to provide the fairest possible competition.

The general public at Devon loves open jumpers and Hackney ponies, and the aficionados are hypnotized by hunters, but there is always a large group of enthusiasts for the Saddlebreds, whooping for a faster rack. The railbirds will swear that their noise and motion contribute something to a flashy

71

performance. Maybe it does, but at any rate it makes things more fun for the spectators.

The three-gaited horses are shown with roached (clipped or shaved) mane and tail, the five-gaited with long and flowing (and sometimes artificial) manes and tails. The high carriage of the five-gaited tail is achieved by surgical nicking and braces, the high action of the legs by training in weights and by different shoes and trimming of the hoof than would be used on hunters or jumpers. It is a rare five-gaited class where the blacksmith is not called into the ring to replace a thrown shoe, a job for which he is allowed seven minutes before the entry is eliminated.

The gaits of the three-gaited Saddlebred are all natural. Those of the five-gaited include two man-made or artificial gaits: the rack, a spectacular four-beat gait in which the horse may reach speeds of thirty miles per hour; and the slow gait, a sort of fox trot. One of the most exciting moments in the ring is when the announcer says "rack on" and the riders let them go. A break into a canter is as disastrous to an exhibitor as to a pacer on the track, but it's a rare occurrence with the caliber of horses at Devon. The five-gaited horse, in addition to his long mane and tail, may also seem somewhat more powerful than the three-gaited because of the extra strength required for the artificial gaits, but both must be strong and "collected" for proper showing. The riders use the posture and long stirrup leathers of dressage, where collection is also all-important. The reins are held very high.

Saddlebreds, whether three-gaited, five-gaited or shown in harness with a four-wheeled show wagon, are a peculiarly American institution, evolved from the walkers of Southern plantation days. Their foundation sires are Tom Hal, a Canadian pacer foaled in 1806, and Denmark, a thoroughbred racehorse who sired Gaines Denmark on "the Stevenson Mare." Gaines Denmark, noted as an officer's charger during the Civil War, is the ancestor of most of today's Saddlebreds. In the behind-the-scenes horse trading that goes on at Devon, a top-flight Saddlebred may change hands for as much as $50,000.

Behind a show wagon, the Saddlebred brings back memories of country fair match races. The horses are shown with a full mane and undocked tail, at three gaits: a walk, a park trot (a high, animated gait in which extreme speed is penalized), and a fast trot assumed on the command, "Show your horse!"—a command which is never given in classes for ladies, juniors or amateurs. Part of the fun in these and other driving classes are the antics performed by the handlers who come racing into the ring to make their charges stand in appropriately heroic attitudes as the judge makes his rounds.

The Saddlebreds sometimes appear to be as high strung as the Hackney ponies—who make a cat on a hot tin roof look somnolent—but with a good rider who manages to keep all of that excitement under control, the tension becomes a source of power and the class can become one of the most thrilling and aesthetically pleasing of the show.

Speaking of aesthetics, riders of Saddlebreds in early shows could wear no colored linings. Three-gaited riders wore a brown or gray riding suit and a bowler. In the evening, riders in both events were expected to wear a black habit, preferably with a boiled shirt, and a high silk hat. In harness classes, however, a high silk hat was never worn; the headgear was always a bowler. After seeing some of the more exuberant outfits on present-day riders, some observers have concluded that a return to the "good old days" might improve the classes by allowing the spectators to concentrate more on the horses.

72

Noted saddlebred trainer Walter Graham at Devon in 1941.

Costume and tack for saddle seat equitation are more subdued than those of the adult classes in this division. An almost military alertness marks the young riders in a saddle seat equitation class.

Five-gaited saddle horse Treasured Possession "racks on."

Venus in Grey, winner of the three-gaited saddle horse class for junior exhibitors, lives up to her name.

Novice harness ponies line up for judging on a newly-raked ring.

Hackneys, Hackney Ponies & Harness Ponies

If you look at the Devon insignia on the program, the officials' medals or the show souvenirs, you will see a handsome small horse at the trot, one foreleg raised high, like the corresponding off hind, neck arched and poll vertical. He is a Hackney, the sports car of our great grandfathers; the one on the seal is Dr. Thomas Ashton's Wynnewood.

The Hackney was bred for speed and brilliance in the English countries of Suffolk and Norfolk during the eighteenth century. The breed also has endurance. One of them, Nonpareil, trotted a measured one hundred miles, farther than the distance from Philadelphia to New York, in about three minutes under ten hours.

The most important sire of the Hackney breed was the thoroughbred Blaze, a grandson of the Darley Arabian, who was bred to both Suffolk Cob and Norfolk Trotter mares to produce the British Hackney coach horse—with speed, quality and great finish,

but smaller (about 15 hands) and lighter than the draft horse dams.

The development of today's popular Hackney pony, ranging from 12 to 13 hands in height, is a result of crossing the Hackney with Welsh ponies. These little animals are too nervous and excitable to be used very much outside the show ring, but are tremendously attractive and far outnumber their big brothers in the classes at Devon.

Spirited Antics

In 1975, Devon supplied a Hackney pony show wagon to transport Bobby Riggs and Richie Ashburn to the mound for a Phillies pre-game exhibition. The driver and the pony, however, had never seen each other except for an hour's practice on foot before the game. Ashburn and Riggs entered the wagon with some trepidation after watching typical

Fine harness pony.

Hackney pony antics—kicking, prancing and rearing—as he waited to go.

An exchange between Devon passenger and celebrity: "Is this thing safe?"

"I don't know, I've never been in one before."

The usually talkative Riggs said not a word on the journey under the stands and around the field. The driver had sent a handler racing ahead to the mound, because Hackney ponies, once they get going, don't like to stop without assistance. But the handler got lost in the maze under Vet Stadium. The wagon ended up circling the diamond and the welcoming committee, one of whom finally served as a groom to bring the equipage to a halt.

The ponies at Devon are usually better known to their drivers and the handlers also know their business, making the classes a bit calmer. But every once in a while, one of them

80

will take it into his head to kick his wagon into toothpicks or drag his driver through the mud, if the handlers unhitch the cart before the bridle.

In 1975, Hackney horse classes were reinstated at Devon after a hiatus caused by the small number of exhibitors. Only a few farms in the United States and Canada now breed the larger animals. The first class for large Hackneys (over 15.2) on Memorial Day, 1975, was filled entirely by Canadian farms. A later class the same day, for Hackneys under 15.2 hands, included several domestic entries.

Nine competitions for Hackneys were held during the week, not counting the four-in-hand driving events—some of the best teams in the latter were also made up of Hackneys. The Canadian exhibitors cleaned up. An American horse, Prince Carlingford Ballantrae (Hawthorne Melody Farm, Liber-

In the fine harness horse class for three-year-olds, ability to stand quietly is a must.

tyville, Illinois), won in only a single class, for a Hackney horse shown to a gig. The $1000 Hackney horse championship went to Outwood Matire, an aged Chestnut gelding (Kilreen Farms, Kars, Ontario), and reserve to Hurstwood Toreador of Glen Lawrence Farm (Kingston, Ontario).

The fifteen classes for Hackney ponies, as usual, were well filled. The best novice pony under 13 hands was a four-year-old brown gelding, Reedann's Star Commander, owned by Leonard P. Cheshire, Alexandria, Virginia. In the novice classes over 13 hands, Ka-Lu-Gemini Cricket, a nine-year-old gelding owned by Clarence Babcock of Brockville, Ontario, won three blues. The open class and the $1500 Hackney pony stake went to Apollo Sand, a six-year-old bay gelding owned by Mr. and Mrs. Kenneth Wheeler of Keswick, Virginia, and driven by noted trainer Gib Marcucci.

Pony Roadsters

The few classes in the ring where speed counts, outside the timed rounds in the open jumper classes, are those for pony roadsters. The ponies may be of any breed, but must stand less than 12.2 hands high. The ponies are shown, with long mane and tail, to a spoke-wheeled bike similar to that used in trotting races, at a trot, road gait, and finally at speed, and they are judged on performance, speed, quality and manners. Although they don't move quite as fast nowadays as when they were shown in former classes outside the ring, they are flashy enough to make the four classes in this division an exciting spectacle, especially when there are sixteen bikes in the ring. Dr. and Mrs. James S. Wolf's noted Midnight Fascination won the class in 1973 and 1974, but the

81

Vehicles drawn by Hackneys at Devon have shown almost as much evolution as the automobile since 1912.

Suspension. A speeding pony roadster is captured at the instant the pony has all four feet off the ground.

pony was not entered this year and first place went to Holly Hocks, a bay mare owned by Mr. and Mrs. Franklin Groves, Wazzata, Minnesota. Terry Jean's Starlight, T. H. White, Jr., Ft. Lauderdale, Florida, placed; for show there was Wild Mustard, a spicy bay gelding owned by Mrs. Bea Hurdman, Ottawa, Ontario, which also picked up blues in two of the three previous classes.

Ponies in the harness pony division are the same size as those shown to roadsters (12.2 hands maximum) and are also shown in long mane and tail, in contrast to the Hackney ponies, which are shown with braided manes and short tails. Conceivably, a Hackney pony could be shown in the harness division, but no ponies may show in both divisions. Most registered harness ponies are a cross of Welsh pony stallions

with Shetland mares, but Shetland-Hackney crosses are also shown.

In contrast to the pony roadster division, the harness ponies are shown to a four-wheeled vehicle, a viceroy or miniature siderail buggy of the type used for fine harness horses, and excessive speed is penalized.

In the harness pony division, Devon was definitely Albelarm Farm's show. Its El Toro won the harness pony open on Monday, Debbie's Fashion the amateur-to-drive class on Wednesday, Dun Haven Daydream the lady's driving class on Thursday and the amateur stake on Friday, and El Toro the harness pony championship on Saturday night. In both the open and the championship class, reserve went to Top Hat, 1974 champion.

In the last analysis, the breeding classes at Devon, held since 1896, may be the most important of all. This is a thoroughbred yearling, suitable to become a hunter.

En pointe. Juan Rieckenhoff's Casanova stretches at the instant of takeoff.

Wow, winning intermediate jumper, hoists the flag like his famous
predecessor Nautical, "The Horse with the Flying Tail."

Devon's best rider of 1975, Rodney Jenkins, always looks for the next fence.

All alone. Quick Decision and his rider become a single competitor on the
isolation of the hunter course.

Inaudible just leaving the ground in the amateur-owner jumper stake.

Powerful impulsion is evident in every muscle of this
champion American saddlebred.

The Hunter Classes

Hunters and Jumpers were once the "poor relations" at Devon, compared to the aristocratic Hackneys and fine harness horses. Most of the entries from the large number of hunt clubs west of Philadelphia were working hunters, shown over difficult courses that tested their ability to jump the kind of fences found in the hunting field. While many, even then, were thoroughbreds for speed, a good crossbred was often in the ribbons, especially in the heavyweight division.

The type of early Devon competition can still be seen at autumn hunter trials in the lovely Chester County countryside, as individual fox hunters ride their mounts at the beginning of hunting season over long outside courses, and the clubs—Radnor, Rose Tree, Pickering, Bellwood, Mr. Stewart's Cheshire Hounds and others—enter members in the team (three) and pair classes. If you're lucky, you may even see a "Tally-ho," in which individual riders compete against

the clock over a hunter course—once also a popular event at Devon. The riders usually own their own horses and, while thoroughbreds predominate at the more posh shows, somebody's nonregistered field hunter can often capture a respectable number of ribbons, provided his performance is good enough.

No longer at Devon. Gone is the outside course with its water jump, its stone wall and its speed classes. Gone too are fences so high that any hunter who got around the course without smashing up too much timber could win a ribbon. The hunters no longer double as jumpers, the number of classes for hunt teams has dwindled, and the thoroughbred reigns.

Pure Show Hunters

Today there are more hunters at Devon than ever before, but in an ironic twist of evolution, the hunter classes—like the Hackney and fine harness events—are now judged for

Sandra Caldwell and Lemon Springs, Devon amateur owner-rider hunter champion, 1975.

beauty and elegance rather than for sheer athletic ability. The latter is left to the open jumpers.

Those who recall the old days vividly think that the hunters have "turned chicken." The fences are lower, the intervals easy, and nobody takes risks the way they used to. Yet the riders are as good or better than they used to be; they will take risks when necessary, and out in the hunting field most of them would rather die than lose the hounds.

But then they aren't riding the same horses.

Pure show hunters are hard to imagine in the field, plunging through briars, scrambling over collapsed stone walls, galloping on paved roads or jumping five-bar gates. They are meant for showing and nothing else. Some of them may have to ride with a recognized hunt a certain number of times to qualify for a working hunter class, but if they do, their riders take *very* good care of them. For a real run with the hounds, Mr. Jorrocks

will brush off a field hunter who has probably never been near a show ring.

The reason, then, that hunter courses may have become a little bland is the same one that prevents most thoroughbred owners from entering a tough steeplechase like the Maryland or Pennsylvania Hunt Cup: economics. No one wants to risk an animal that may be worth $100,000 over courses with teeth in them.

What the hunter classes may have lost in raw excitement, however, they have made up in subtlety, finesse and poetry in motion. To many people, horsemen and spectators alike, a conformation hunter (judged on physical perfection as well as performance) is the aristocrat of the equine world. The finest of past years at Devon, such as Duke of Paeonian, Cold Climate, Waiting Home, and the unbeatable Cap and Gown, had the combination of solidity and flowing line one sees in the portraits of Solarion.

Until recently, hunters were divided

Moreno has "propped"–taken off too close to the fence–in an owner-to-ride class for local working hunters.

The result (above) is a sharp jolt on take-off and a hard landing that almost unseats the rider. But an arm on the right side helps her back to complete the round.

A green conformation hunter (Southern Square), in spite of only one year's show experience, illustrates the proper arc over a fence.

into light, medium and heavyweight classifications, a distinction that became too difficult to make as the number of hunter classes increased.

Hunter classes in general are broken into two major types: working hunters, judged solely on performance; and conformation hunters, judged on performance plus quality. In green conformation hunter classes (for horses with less than two years' show experience), performance counts half and conformation half. As the horse gains more experience and becomes a regular conformation hunter, performance counts 60 percent.

Working hunters are also divided into green and regular sections. The first-year green working hunter section was omitted for the first time in the 1975 show. Second year greens, horses in their second year of showing, still appear in large numbers.

There are also several subspecies of hunter classes. In the Corinthian Class, the appointments of horse and rider are also scored. The same is true of appointments and hunt team classes. In these, the rider must wear traditional fox hunting attire. He must also wear spurs and carry a hunting whip, a spare pair of rain gloves under the girth, and an appropriate sandwich case and flask attached to the saddle. The judge checks each of these items, including the contents of the sandwich case and the flask (sherry or brandy). In the Corinthian Class, the rider must also be an amateur and a bona fide member of a recognized hunt, wearing its formal livery.

Junior hunters, ridden by exhibitors under eighteen, are shown under regular working hunter conditions with slightly lower fences. The same is true of pony hunters ridden by junior exhibitors and divided into classes for ponies (14.2 hands and under), small ponies (13.0 hands and under) and tiny ponies (11.2 hands and under).

Handy hunter classes, for seniors and juniors, test the agility of the horse by setting a course requiring tight turns, jumping from tricky take-off positions and other tight spots a rider might encounter during an actual hunt.

Devon also has classes for local working hunters, horses owned by exhibitors living within a fifty-mile radius of Devon; for amateur owners, in which the entry must be ridden by the owner or a member of his immediate family; and a number of "outlaw" classes. These are classes that do not meet AHSA specifications, but because of tradition or intrinsic interest are still run, even though the horse does not receive any points toward the show championship or AHSA standing. These include the Chappaqua Challenge Trophy for lady's hunter, sidesaddle; Mr. Newbold Ely's Hounds Challenge Trophy; the Better Days Challenge Trophy for best hunter-hack combination horse; and the Kimberton Hills Farm Trophy for young hunters under saddle. The hunter-hack class is an interesting mixture—the horses are driven into the ring hitched to a vehicle such as a dog cart or a shooting brake, judged for suitability and appointments, unharnessed and saddled. The driver then mounts and rides a program that includes walk, trot and canter, hand gallop, backing and fast stop, and a few fences. The horses are judged on performance, suitability, appointments and ease in switching from one role to another. The class in 1975 was won by Mrs. F. E. Whaley on Pumpkin, who also won it in 1974.

At every large show there is usually a "dumping" class, that is, one that many people enter without any intention of showing. For the entry fee, they obtain exhibitor privileges that are worth the price of a single fee. As entries come in, the show managers always try to spot the fake class, which changes every year, so that they can put a stop to it. In 1975, they thought it would be the lady's sidesaddle class, in which entries really piled up, but at show time they were surprised to find all forty-two entries in the ring.

Perhaps because of the nostalgia craze, the sidesaddle has lately become something of a fad. Its proponents claim that it is more secure and comfortable, besides being more proper for a lady than a cross saddle. With apologies, the ladies in the ring on Thursday night weren't very good at it; they had trouble jumping a couple of very low fences and they didn't post the trot, but they did look very chic. Maybe performance will improve with practice. In the meantime, they might remember what Lida Fleitman Bloodgood, one of the best, has pointed out: that a sidesaddle on a rearing horse is a convenient form of suicide. With one leg clamped around the horn it's hard to bail out fast enough.

Subtlety of Style

The hunter and hunter breeding judges ostensibly look for jumping ability, manners, style, pace and quality—a horse that would be a safe, comfortable ride in the hunt field, with the stamina for a long day's hunting and the manners to make it enjoyable. On these qualities alone, all the horses entered at Devon could have been given a blue ribbon.

What they were actually looking for was considerably more subtle, but not beyond the grasp of anyone taking the time to look closely at each of the seemingly endless rounds of the hunter classes. Each fence is scored, in a kind of shorthand, on the judges' cards. The flight should be a perfect arc, of a length proportional to the height of the fence, beginning

90

Lines of this thoroughbred yearling belie the old saw about four white feet.

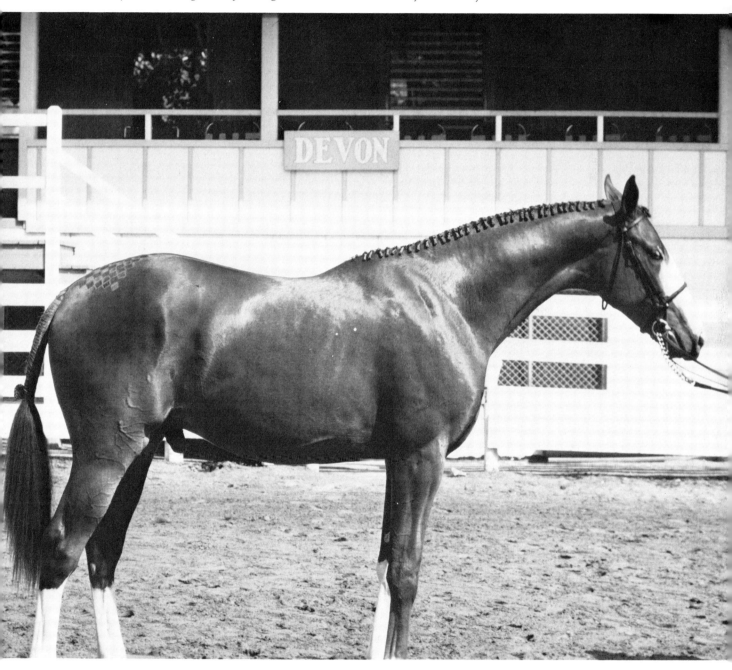

Given half a chance, a hunter can always find a place to graze.

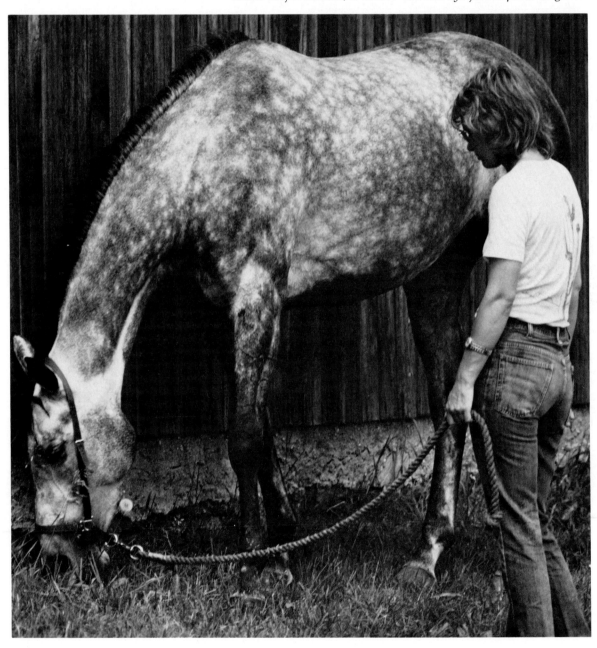

and ending equidistant from the obstacle. Thus "propping," or taking off too close to the fence, taking off too far away, or diving (jumping with too flat a trajectory) would all be penalized. So would hesitation in front of a fence; "weaving," in which the attempts of the horse to duck out or refuse to jump must continually be corrected by the rider; any change in pace between the fences; misbehavior, such as bucking; or a lack of form in the air, such as letting one leg hang down or not tucking up the forelegs sufficiently.

People accustomed to AHSA jumping rules sometimes attach too much importance to "ticks," which can be heard when a hoof just touches the rail of a fence. All other things being equal, a tick is a fault in a hunter class, but a horse with all good arcs over fences may be scored higher than one that completes a round without any ticks because he is jumping too high for the size of the fence. A tick caused by a jumping fault, however, definitely rates a demerit.

Even with all these variables, it may be hard to choose among the rounds in the best classes at Devon. With such subtlety of distinction, little things become very important, such as the judge's opinion of a proper hunting pace, the slightest deviation from a true course to the middle of each fence or the willingness of the horse.

Taking a hunter through a perfect round requires a great deal of skill and experience. Most of the riders in open working and conformation classes are now professionals, such as Rodney Jenkins, Dave Kelley, Bernie Traurig or Vince Dugan, who can rate horses so that they take off at exactly the right point, maintain a perfectly regular pace and make the horse look as if he enjoyed it. Such women as Carol Hoffman, Michele McEvoy, Mary Chapot, Terri Rudd and many others familiar on the show circuit are as good as, if not better than, the men in maintaining the kind of rapport that shows a hunter to best advantage.

Memorial Day at Devon was heaven for hunter enthusiasts. In the Gold Ring at 11:00 A.M., there were thirty-six second-year green working hunters; in the Wanamaker Oval that afternoon, there were two divisions of open model (shown in-hand, not under saddle) green conformation hunters—nineteen in A division and seventeen in B. There were also combination hunter-hack, working hunters, open and working hunters under saddle (no fences), and open model *regular* conformation hunters. Horses from thirty-one states, including San Felipe from Puerto Rico—this year's reserve champion working hunter—competed.

But they were just getting warmed up. The only champion hunter to win a blue that day was the Meadowland Stables' Velvet Tux, ridden to victory in the second-year green working hunter division by Rodney Jenkins. Eastern Shore, Cismont Manor Farms, and Mrs. R. Huffines' champion in the green conformation A division, came in second in the model class. Mrs. John Gaston's Cool Shoes, ridden by Bernie Traurig to the B division championship, could only manage a fifth in the model class. Tanrackin Farm's Royal Reveler, regular conformation hunter champion, got second in his model class; Winter Place Farm's superb Gozzi, working hunter and grand hunter champion of Devon, placed second to Winter Place's Royal Blue in the regular working hunter under saddle.

Class tells in the long run and a week at Devon is a long run for any hunter. By championship day on Saturday, Velvet Tux was the champion green working hunter, with Erdenheim Farm's Columbia, Michael Matz up, reserve. Eastern Shore and Cool

93

A good fence for Air Fare in the regular working hunter class for the Thomas W. Clark Memorial Challenge Trophy.

George Morris, one of the best known hunter riders at Devon, has also trained many Junior exhibitors.

Shoes had won the first and second-year green conformation hunter titles and Royal Reveler had amassed 21½ points with three wins and ribbons in three additional classes, to take the regular conformation hunter crown. Vital Victory was reserve. Gozzi was the undisputed working hunter and grand hunter champion, with 26 points.

A Palomino, Lemon Springs, ridden by Sandra Caldwell, was champion of the local working hunters for the second consecutive year and also won the amateur owner championship. Another Palomino, Sky High, was reserve in the local working hunter section.

Wickas' Warlock, ridden by Joan Kelly, won the lady's hunter sidesaddle class. The Newbold Ely trophy went to Columbia, with a second to Mr. and Mrs. Mark Herr's Shredni, ridden by Vince Dugan, and the Kimberton Hills Farm trophy for young hunters under saddle went to Stand Up and Cheer, owned by Mrs. Peter Platten and Cismont Manor Farms, Keswick, Virginia.

95

Rider's position, while unorthodox, gives the horse plenty of freedom. Contact is maintained with the fingertips.

Don't look down. Michele McEvoy on Sundancer during the open jumper stake for the U.S.E.T. Challenge Trophy.

Open Jumpers

The $1000 Devon Invitational Open Jumper Stake on Sunday was the opening round in a seesaw battle among the country's leading open jumpers that raged until the last event on the last night of the show. The difficult courses, designed by the noted British course designer, Pamela Carruthers, brought out the best in such champion open horses as Idle Dice, Sundancer, A Little Bit, Antar, Mighty Ruler, Don Juan, Number One Spy, Caesar and Space Citation, and the competition was the closest in years. The same was true of the intermediate and the new amateur-owner jumper divisions.

The Sunday class was an indication of things to come, turning into a speed duel between Number One Spy, ridden by Rodney Jenkins, and A Little Bit, with Buddy Brown. A good number of horses jumped the tricky course with its 5-foot heights and 7-foot spreads without faults, in both the first round and the timed first jump-off, so

seconds spelled the difference between victory and defeat. Number One Spy completed the course in 36.479 to win the class; A Little Bit took second with a time of 38.661. Space Citation was third.

Sentimental Favorite

On Monday night in the same type of class, sponsored by the Pennsylvania Horsemen's Association, the order was reversed, with A Little Bit winning in a time of 35.006 to Number One Spy's 35.842. Sundancer, ridden by Michelle McEvoy, came back to take third, after being out of the money on Sunday. Idle Dice, the sentimental favorite and one of the best jumping horses this country has ever produced, placed seventh in the first event and fifth in the second.

The jumpers at Devon are an anomaly. Evolved long ago from the events for green working hunters into the AHSA "rub

Rodney Jenkins, leading rider at Devon in 1975, is usually close to a sure thing in the Gambler's Choice.

classes," and finally into the easy-to-score Table II events, where only knock-downs or refusals count, they are now the most popular of all with the general public. They are also the only classes at the show where sheer performance counts. It makes not the slightest bit of difference what the horse looks like, how the rider sits, what he wears or how he holds the reins, as long as the horse gets over the fence. He can give it a good rap with forefoot or hind foot, knock off a rail or set the whole thing rocking, but as long as the height or spread (width of the obstacle) is not changed, he is not faulted.

Most of the open jumpers at Devon, as at other major shows, are thoroughbreds, a good proportion of them off the track, but any breed can be entered. Looks don't count and neither does pedigree: only athletic ability. (The Germans, with their customary thoroughness, are now breeding horses along

the lines of kangaroos, especially for show jumping.)

The courses they jump consist of a variety of obstacles—crossed poles; triple bars; a spread of three obstacles of progressively greater height; oxers, with the highest element in the middle; railroad crossing gates; simulated stone walls and so on—but the difficulty of the course depends more upon its design than the height or type of the obstacles, which are relatively standard. The designer may devise an in-and-out or triple, a set of two or three related fences, so that a horse may have to put in one very long or two short strides between each element, making it harder to choose the correct takeoff point; provide difficult turns into straight up-and-down fences, harder to judge than spreads; or even create psychological obstacles, such as having the last approach away from the gate by which the horse expects to leave the ring.

100

A rare moment of calm in a hackney pony class as ponies pose for the judges.

Jewel-box splendor of tack rooms remains untouched throughout the show.

A young hopeful in the mare and foal class may return as an adult competitor.

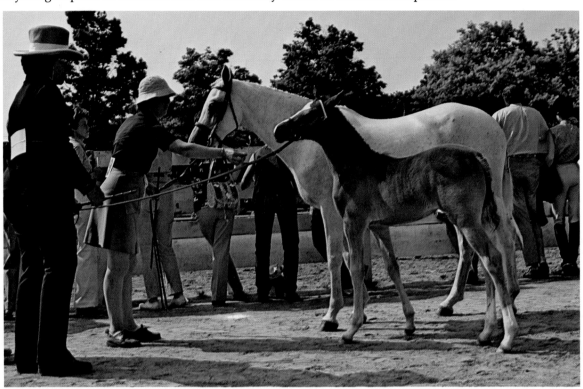

Devon is one of the few shows in the world with four-in-hand
driving competitions.

The Main Line Midway. Promenade in front of the main grandstand leads an
afternoon crowd to the Devon Country Fair.

Forelegs well tucked up, an intermediate jumper clears an obstacle in the fault-and-out class. Object is to jump as many fences as possible within a fixed time limit.

Rodney Jenkins entered his own gelding, Y Hugo, in the intermediate jumper classes. In this one he took third.

Carol Hofmann Thompson, one of the country's leading female riders, takes Mrs. Leonard King's Tara Hill over an intermediate jumper course.

Fort Knox stretches for one in an intermediate jumper fault-and-out class.

Before any open jumping event, you will see all the riders pacing the course, pacing off the intervals, kicking takeoff points and otherwise trying to guess what new deviltry the designer has been up to this time. The object is to produce a course that *some,* but not all, can jump clean, and which will still be viable if shortened and raised for a jump-off.

Major Jumping Events

There are three main types of jumping events at Devon: for open jumpers, horses that have won more than $3000 during their careers; for intermediate jumpers, which have won less than $3000; and for amateur owners, jumpers of any classification ridden by an amateur owner or member of the owner's immediate family. Until recently, there were also classes for green or preliminary jumpers, which had won $1000 or less, but these have gradually been phased out with the growth of the open and intermediate divisions.

The horses compete in a variety of events governed by AHSA rules. Table I events (rub classes), in which the horses are scored by a system of faults for front or hind touches, knock-downs or refusals, are seldom seen at larger shows now, except in the Junior Jumper Division. Most of the classes are scored under various sections of AHSA Table II. Basically, the rules for Table II classes are the same as those for Table I, except that touches are not penalized. Each knock-down counts as four faults, each refusal or disobedience (failure to jump the obstacle) counts three faults, and three refusals eliminates. In most classes a maximum time to complete the course is calculated; any horse exceeding that time is penalized one-quarter fault for every second or fraction of a second by which the time is exceeded. A fall by the horse or rider eliminates in most (not all) events, as will various mistakes such as failure to enter the ring within one minute of being called. In the first two classes described above (time first jump-off), the first round is scored by adding jumping and time faults. In the jump-off or second round, for horses that have gone clean or without faults in the first, the time taken to complete the course decides between any two horses with clean rounds or equal jumping faults.

The open jumpers have become such a popular attraction at Devon that one such class is usually scheduled each night. The intermediate and amateur-owner events generally occur during the afternoon in the Gold Ring.

The Tuesday night class—another time first jump-off—was a third duel between Rodney Jenkins and Buddy Brown, this time with Rodney and Number One Spy coming out on top. In a $1500 class, first place pays $450, second $270 and so on, down to eighth, at $75. The open jumper classes at Devon in 1975 offered a total of $12,000 in prize money.

In the Gambler's Choice on Wednesday, Idle Dice showed what he could do. The Gambler's Choice course consists of ten jumps, each marked with a different point value from 10 to 100, depending upon the difficulty. The rider can choose whatever fence he wants, providing none are jumped more than twice, and is credited with the points marked on every fence jumped clean within the time allowed (usually less than a minute). Ties are decided on the basis of time.

Idle Dice won the event with a total of 800 points, a credit both to his jumping ability and to Rodney Jenkins's genius for choosing the shortest line between the two most valuable points. Rodney Jenkins, the closest to a superstar that the show jumping circuit has yet produced, seems almost a throwback to the day of Freddy Wettach. His style is unorthodox, but it gets the most out of whatever horse he is riding. Tall and gangling with an unruly thatch of red hair, he never seems to hurry. Idle Dice, too, appears to loaf along at an easy canter and it is not until you see his time, compared to horses that scramble around at breakneck speed, that you realize how fast he is moving, how well Rodney has calculated the course and how many corners he has cut. Sometimes corner cutting gets him into spots tight enough to make the crowd gasp, but he has an uncanny ability to make Idle Dice, Antar, or Number One Spy jump clean from the most impossible-looking take-off points.

Idle Dice, a big (17.2) brown gelding, twelve years old in 1975, has a deceptive turn of speed. He raced as a two-and three-year-old, was trained as a hunter, and finally was sold to Harry Gill of Malvern, who trained him as a jumper. He has won over $100,000 on the show jumping circuit, competed successfully against the best in international competition, won the President's Cup twice, and cleared a height of 7 feet, 2¾ inches, in the puissance at the Washington, D.C., International. From the cheers that greeted his victory in the Gambler's Choice at Devon, it was clear that the fans wanted him to remain the best show jumper in the United States.

The Cardinal, ridden by Bernie Traurig, took second place with 780 points; Caesar, Joe Fargis up, also had 780 points but a slightly slower time.

In the fault and out on Thursday, speed and brilliance paid off, however, as Michele McEvoy rode Sundancer, a fast, compact and highly excitable chestnut with four white stockings, to a victory over Idle Dice by 2 points. The fault and out takes place over medium-size obstacles (4–4½ feet), each of which is numbered. The rider's round finishes with the first fault—knock-down or refusal—or when the course is completed clean in the time allowed. Two points are scored for each fence jumped clean and one for a knock-down. If an obstacle is knocked down, or the time is up, the horn sounds and the horse must jump the next fence. The clock is stopped as soon as the forefeet touch the ground. Michele, going hell for leather, picked up 28 points. All of the other ribbon winners had 26, and were placed in order of time, Idle Dice followed by The Cardinal, Number One Spy and Mighty Ruler.

Michelle is one of the best in the up-and-coming generation of new riders, and her win on Sundancer might have been the result of sheer guts and determination. She proved that it was no fluke by winning the USET Challenge Trophy the following night. This class was the only one at Devon this year held under FEI rules, basically the same as the Table II time first jump-off classes, but with riders carrying a minimum weight of 175 pounds, and falls penalized by eight faults instead of elimination. Sundancer jumped both rounds clean, the second in 36.4 seconds, one-tenth of a second faster than the runner-up, Don Juan, another fast-moving performer. A Little Bit was third and Idle Dice fourth. Nine horses with an equal number of faults were tied for eighth place.

The $5000 open jumper stake on closing night was an upset. Maybe it was a case of endurance. The class was the last in the show and it included a time *second* jump-off, meaning that horses putting in two clean rounds within the allotted time then jumped a *third* round against the clock in a driving rainstorm. At any rate, it was Rodney Jenkins's third ride, Meadowland Stables' Antar, who could do no better than fourth all week, who won the class. Another long shot, Samba, owned by W. C. Boren III and ridden by Noel Twyman, finished second. Grande

106

Melanie Smith winning her first class at Devon during 1975 on Crimson Tide, intermediate jumper champion.

Amateur-owner jumping events were new at Devon in 1975. This is Robert Thomas' Battle Flags from Tampa, Florida.

was third, Don Juan fourth, Idle Dice fifth and Aries sixth. Number One Spy and A Little Bit were out of the ribbons, but both of them had picked up 14 points in other classes, making them joint champions. Rodney Jenkins received the tri-colored sash of the leading open jumper rider early in the week and later took home the trophy for the sixth time at Devon, with a total of 35½ points.

Most of the riders in the open jumper classes are professionals, riding for a single large stable or for other owners at a fixed fee per ride. Some, like Michelle McEvoy and Juan Rieckehoff, are owner riders. The proportion of owner riders rises in the intermediate jumper classes—Rodney Jenkins, for example, rode his own horse, Y Hugo—and reaches 100 percent in the amateur owner classes. The intermediate classes, with their restrictions on amount of prize money won, give a chance to relative newcomers, but the successful are usually the new contenders in the open classes. The intermediate jumpers in 1975 were dominated by Crimson Tide, owned by Stillmeadow Farm and ridden by Melanie Smith. Crimson Tide won two events, finished second in another and third in the stakes class, for a winning score of 15 points. Y Hugo and Johnny's Pocket tied for reserve with 10 points each.

Amateur owner-jumper classes were held for the first time at Devon in 1975, with such success that they will certainly be a fixture of shows to come. The classes were well filled and the events, if less polished, were almost as exciting as the big open classes held under the lights, even if the fences were not quite as high, nor the intervals designed by Pamela Carruthers quite as demanding. At the end of the week, Vesuvius, owned by Doc Severinson's Harmony Farm and ridden by Alan Severinson, was the Champion; Tinker Toy, owned by Mrs. Carleton Blunt, was reserve. Also winning blues were War Machine, Robin Neuberger, and Red Road, August A. Busch, Jr.

The manager of the Devon Horse Show has the prerogative of riding on a coach-and-four, which is fun even in a cloudburst.

Main Line Midway:

The Devon Country Fair

A microcosm of Philadelphia Society, the Country Fair is industrious, cheerful, first-rate, unflappable and very profitable, but interesting things, in the sense of the bizarre, the scandalous or the unpredictable, simply never happen. They are not allowed to.

The fair and the horse show are like an old married couple, bickering but inseparable. Under different managements they drift closer or further apart, but neither one could do without the other.

The Country Fair did not spring full-blown from the brow of Mrs. Archibald Barklie in 1919. She and Mrs. Charlton Yarnall had organized a similar affair for the Emergency Aid of Pennsylvania during 1917, and many of the ladies who had served on those fund-raising committees went to work in support of Bryn Mawr Hospital when the war ended. Others had served on the Board of Lady Visitors of the Bryn Mawr Hospital.

The incorporation of the Devon Horse

Show and Country Fair in 1919 formalized events that had been going on at Devon for many years. The cafeteria, for example, had grown out of shared luncheon dishes, and impromptu dances had been held on a hardwood floor laid on the turf near the bandstand. The crowd, like that at Ascot, was a fashion show in itself.

The first Country Fair, although its work took place entirely during the show, had almost as many events as the current version and several hundred committee members, most of whom were the wives of men associated with the horse show or directors of Bryn Mawr Hospital.

From the beginning, the fair made money. In 1919 it donated $26,000 to the hospital. Every item it sold was donated, from the devilled eggs in the cafeteria to the cigars in the tobacco shop. Most of the committee women had large gardens, not to mention gardeners, and the fruit and vegetable booth

111

"Gone are the thatch-roofed cottages..." but the Devon Country Fair remains.

*From the top of the ferris wheel the midway
stretches toward Devon's east grandstand.*

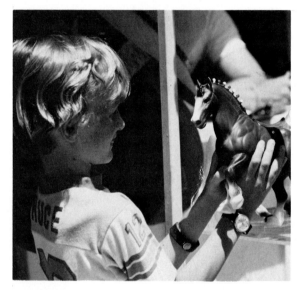

*Even children who have the real thing like to
collect models at Devon's "Paper Pony."*

*Candy apples and cotton candy are equally
sticky.*

was stocked with pecks and bushels of produce in season and a veritable Covent Garden of flowers. People knitted, tatted and crocheted, and the products of their labor were donated and sold.

Another reason the fair made money was that each committee competed with the others to see which could make the greatest contribution to the hospital, a technique that has survived to this day.

The committee chairmen had a considerable degree of autonomy, or if they didn't have it, they took it. There were no by-laws. Any money required by an individual committee for its work at the fair was usually raised by its own pre-show events, beginning the custom of year-round fund raising that prevails today.

Mrs. Horace B. Hare, a noted fox hunter, suggested that a prize fight might bring in quite a lot of money, "provided it was a real fight that the working men would be interested in" ("and could bet on," *crossed out in the original minutes*). She agreed to look into it. At the next meeting, it was reported that a Mr. Gunnis had agreed to put on a professional fight for $1000, but the committee decided against the offer unless given a percentage of the gate.

Starting with Mrs. Hare's abortive prize fight, the fair has always been innovative in its fund-raising events. (It's been conservative too, sometimes. Cigarette machines were prohibited on the grounds in 1935 because they "attracted a bad element" and the prohibition has stood ever since.)

All of this activity, including donated radio time, auctions and parades, resulted in ever-increasing donations to the hospital. In 1956, everyone scrambled to raise $60,000 for the show's sixtieth anniversary. In 1974, the fair donated $140,000, and in 1975, $145,000.

Since 1919, Bryn Mawr has received well over $2.5 million in donations from the fair alone, helping to make it one of the best equipped and staffed hospitals in the East.

Time Stood Still

The events at the Country Fair itself have not changed very much. There is still the fifty-five-year-old candy booth (rebuilt this year) with homemade fudge and that peculiar Philadelphia institution, a lemon pierced with a stick of hard candy through which the lucky or the skillful can suck the juice. The same well-dressed little girls parade through the crowds with their wares, making half the sales of the booth on the days when it doesn't rain. The tea house has been converted to an antique shop, one of the most successful of last year's enterprises, but old timers still ask for the landmark tea house. Iced tea with mint and little tea sandwiches are now sold from a cart with a blue-striped awning. The tea cart is still supplied from the old tea house kitchen, known as the "beauty shop" because of the steam treatment provided by brewing hundreds of gallons of tea on a hot day, and the effect on the hands of slicing ten cases of lemons. The meals are now catered. The ladies in the information booth still announce lost children, sell Devon trinkets and answer the phone calls: "When is the next race?" The hospital shop sells items handcrafted by volunteers throughout the year and the hot dog booth sells 10,000 hot dogs, 2,600 hoagies and 6,000 soft pretzels. Devon-goers, however, seem to prefer hamburgers and the sandwich booth served 13,472 during the last show, plus 22,300 ice cream cones and 55,000 soft drinks.

On the promenade, the stroller can still buy fashionable clothes, hats, leather goods, Ferraris or works of art from many boutiques

The old Devon Tea House has become a booth, but on a hot day it still attracts both riders and spectators.

set up by Philadelphia's best stores, splurge on a horsey gewgaw at the Fox Room, or buy serious riding equipment at one of three tack shops.

Over toward the stables, the midway begins with a ferris wheel and pony rides leading into an alley of games of skill and chance. Many of these are still staffed by Country Fair volunteers, but all of the rides and games, which at one time were set up by the fair, are now provided by a concessionaire.

Amidst the intense activity is the war room of the Country Fair, an oasis of calm with sepia-toned old photos on the walls, where officers can plot the next day's strategy and committee chairmen can rest frayed nerves. The "Blue Room," which is actually pink, is under the main grandstand and off limits to all but the most exalted of horse show personnel.

115

DEVON HORSE SHOW
DEVON, PENNA.

MAY 27, 28, 29, 31,
LADIES' DAY,
MONDAY, MAY 31, 1914

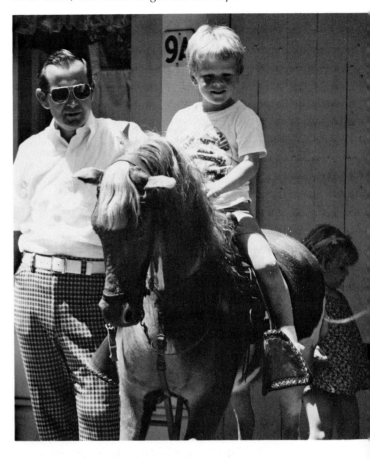

This photographer's model of a pony has a good Arab head, but needs to get his ears up.

The Country Fair, like any enterprise dealing with large numbers of people, has its problems. On WIP days, when the Engelbert Humperdincks of the world appear, the facilities are innundated; the best exhaust fans in the world do not quite eradicate the smell of pizza; the shooting gallery sometimes bothers the horses; but visiting the Country Fair is still a strangely pleasant, almost nostalgic experience, largely because of the people who run it. An expert in foreign exchange who deals daily with the Gnomes of Zurich may be scraping the hamburger grill, while a surgeon serves ice cream and your stockbroker fills balloons: during the week of Devon they are there to serve the public, and they do it with friendliness, courtesy and devotion. Many of the jobs at the fair are hot, arduous and nerve-wracking, but nothing ever upsets the volunteers for very long.

Twins in the exhibitors' stand pay more attention to spun sugar than to what's happening in the ring just in front of them. (Opposite) A show hunter gets his reward.

118

Candy stand is one of the oldest (1919) at the Devon Country Fair.

Colorful clothes, for men and women, are a tradition at Devon.

Champion conformation hunter Royal Reveler can't resist his reflection in the Spindletop Challenge Trophy plate.

Devon Trophies

If the Devon Horse Show and Country Fair ever unloads its silver collection on the open market, the price will decline to $2.40 an ounce. By 1929, Devon was already the most heavily endowed show in the country in terms of trophies, a tradition it maintains today. And these were not the cups and plaques one buys on jewelers' row. The Second Devon Victory Challenge Cup, for the exhibitor winning the largest number of points, was a George III silver coffee urn, circa 1777, by C. Wright, standing 20½ inches high. The Crebilly Challenge Trophy for best junior five-gaited saddle horse was a Sheffield silver tea urn made in 1817. R.R.M. Carpenter's Dilwyne Farm Trophy for best hunt team was another massive silver urn, 1811, by J. W. Story and W. Elliott. The Ruston Challenge Trophy, for ladies' hunters over an

Devon champion for size and ornateness is the John Wanamaker Trophy for the winner of the Open Jumper Stake.

121

The Strawbridge and Clothier Challenge Trophy for open conformation hunters.

The short-tailed saddle horse Gold Leaf won this elegant trophy at Devon in 1912.

The Castleton Farms Challenge Trophy for champion five-gaited saddle horses.

The Thomas W. Clark Memorial Trophy for regular working hunters has been contested since 1944.

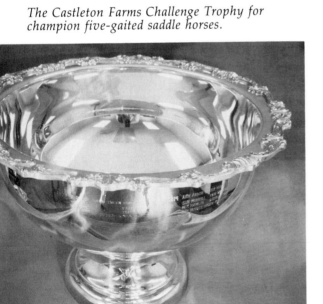

One of the top laurels of Devon's junior Weekend: the Prim and Proper Challenge Trophy for champion pony hunters.

(Opposite) *Changing trophy styles are illustrated by two won by Mrs. J. A. Du Pont prior to World War I (top and center),* compared to the *modern Second Crooked Billet Challenge Trophy (bottom)* for junior jumpers.

outside course, was a huge Victorian silver gilt tankard; the Edward T. Stotesbury Memorial Trophy for Champion lady's hunter, provenance unknown, was the most ornate piece of silver sculpture since Benvenuto Cellini.

Most of these and many other gorgeous trophies have been retired after being won three times by the same exhibitor, but as fast as they are taken home, they are replaced by new pieces. For the most important classes and divisions, there is a waiting list of potential donors, and the collection reposing in the vault at Bailey, Banks and Biddle remains massive. Plate for many of the individual classes is purchased each year. The stored trophies are challenge cups, usually named for a former champion or donated in memory of Devon's best-known exhibitors, officials or supporters. A very few are perpetual trophies, but even challenge trophies usually have a long life, because of the difficulty in winning three consecutive times in any division.

Crebilly's Vanity's Sensation, out of Meadow Vanity, one of the foremost saddlebreds of the fifties.
(Painting by Elizabeth Bell.)

The 356 Days of Preparation

The nine days of the Devon Horse Show and Country Fair demand 356 days of preparation, the work of thousands of volunteers and the expenditure of large amounts of capital. This corporation, large even by American standards, for most of the year is divided into two separate entities that come together for a little more than a week in May. Each of them, the Horse Show and the Country Fair, has its own officers, volunteers, headquarters and paid staff, but they are both controlled by The Devon Horse Show and Country Fair, Inc. The titles of various officers can be confusing, since one person may be simultaneously vice president of the DHS&CF, a member of the Horse Show Committee and a director of the Country Fair. There are two blue-ribbon boards of directors, one for the DHS&CF and one for the Country Fair.

The officers of the DHS&CF are usually members of the Horse Show Committee as well, and the president of the DHS&CF, Richard E. McDevitt, Esq., also presides at the monthly show committee meetings. The Horse Show Committee itself has no officers except the chairman, Mrs. Edgar Scott; what it does have is a plethora of subcommittees, the chairmen of which generally make up the show committee. The committee names may help to summarize a few of the myriad details that become so invisible in May. They are the executive committee, the coordinating committee, the stakes sponsorship committee, trophy and reception committee, the entertainment committee, the ladies' committee, the gentlemen's committee, the Devon Club, Carriage Marathon, catalog advertising, gate and grandstand operations, grounds, judges' reception, public relations, reservations, and special ceremonies. In addition to coordinating the work of several hundred committee members, the chairmen vote in the show committee on matters of general business and may have special jobs as well.

Nearly all of these people are jammed into the basement office of the committee stand for an hour or two each month for the meetings of the Horse Show Committee. Also present will be John J. Burkholder, general manager of the show since the days of Freddy Pinch and James J. Fallon, manager of Devon and assistant manager of the National at Madison Square Garden.

Meetings are short, quiet and casual. Most of the actual work of the show is done in committee, and the first part of the meeting consists of brief reports by each chairman—ribbons (almost 2000) and trophies have been ordered, tickets printed, new glassware purchased for the clubhouse, a roof repaired, subscriptions received for a new barn—routine details that the chairmen and their committees have handled many times before.

If there are any votes, they are usually to approve some action already thoroughly investigated by two committees, the one involved and the executive committee. One such question was the decision to eliminate first-year green working hunters from the 1975 schedule. It provoked some discussion, but everyone was in general agreement that it had to be done. Most decisions are made the same way. There is little factionalism, since everybody knows what has to be done and does it. Arguments may occur about *degrees* of action, seldom over the action itself. Tradition is a more concise guide than a set of bylaws. The atmosphere is that of a discussion among friends, rather than a committee meeting.

126

After the last report, someone breaks out a picnic basket containing bottles, ice, glasses and snacks, and the officer counter becomes a bar for the cocktail hour. The actual meeting has lasted an hour but discussion, sometimes more important than the formalities of the meeting, continues over drinks until about seven.

The New Show Takes Shape

By September the new show, still nine months away, begins to take shape. An eighty-page prize list, containing a schedule and descriptions of 232 classes, will be mailed in March to 2000 prospective exhibitors. By the time that occurs, the committee must have determined what the classes will be, arranged for sponsors, allocated prize money, invited judges (and received their acceptances), and invited a course designer, four stewards, two announcers, three ringmasters and two farriers. Selection of eleven veterinarians is handled by a special veterinary committee under the direction of Mark W. Allam, V.M.D.

Before the show itself, the committee must have hired a security force; arranged with police to handle traffic; hired parking attendants, ticket takers and ushers; rented additional parking space; arranged for a jump crew; bought ribbons and trophies, liquor and souvenirs; printed a 292-page catalog; found suppliers of food and fodder and *two* firms to cart away 250 tons of manure; conducted an advertising and publicity program; set up a schedule of special events; invited the press and honored guests; taken the perpetual and challenge trophies from their storage vault at Bailey, Banks and Biddle, an old Philadelphia jewelry firm; set up 320 temporary stalls in three large tents on the grounds (Devon and another large horse show own the pre-fab

Devon president Richard E. McDevitt, Esq. entertains guests in the committee stand.

A coach horse seems to know what to expect from a hose nozzle.

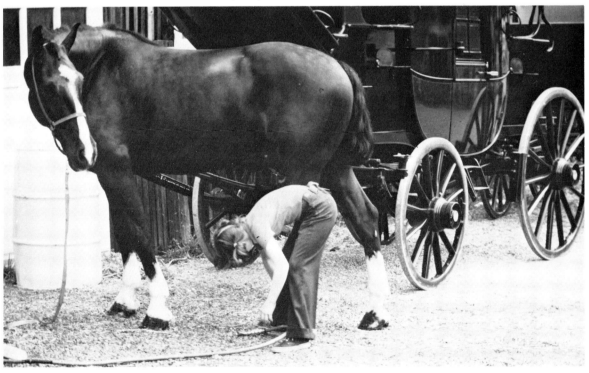

stalls jointly); staff and stock the first-aid headquarters and arrange ambulance service; and perform a thousand other jobs that no one ever thinks about during the course of the show.

At that, Devon is fortunate in some of the things it *doesn't* have to do. The Country Fair allocates the booths and concessions on the grounds and staffs those it runs itself. Parking facilities are adequate, if not generous, compared to those available for a midtown show such as the National. Devon owns its grounds, so it has no rent to pay or over-cautious landlords to contend with. And it has no union problems.

The last Horse Show Committee meeting of the summer is held in June. The only job remaining is the compilation of results required by the AHSA for its records of point standings for individual horses and riders. The results, the size of a minor novel, are compiled by the show's public relations agency, Burbank Associates, from records kept in the press box.

The next meeting will be in September, when preparations will begin again to accelerate toward a new climax. In the meantime, the field is left to the Country Fair, which holds fund-raising events all year long; to Burkholder and Fallon, who maintain exhibitor relations; and to the grounds committee and grounds superintendent Wilmer Fronheiser.

A Year-Round Job

The grounds do not lie idle for fifty-one weeks of the year. They are used for events ranging from the Scottish Games through the Country Fair Tailgate Sale to the Sugartown Horse Show. Until recently, they were also the site of a large dog show, an outgrowth of the Devon Dog Show that once was held simultaneously with the horse show. This show eventually

Time keeper is well-prepared. He is aided nowadays by electronic timers accurate to a hundredth of a second.

Thoroughbred yearling, suitable to become hunter.

became so large that not even Devon's twenty-seven acres could hold it without serious strain and it was moved elsewhere.

The superintendent's responsibility includes not only the grounds, with water pipes close to the surface, recalcitrant drains, fences, roadways and tracks, but also forty-four ancient buildings in the Country Fair Village, twenty-eight barns with 490 permanent stalls and ten horse show buildings. Tours of inspection now take place in a golf cart. They used to be done on a pony.

The mere painting of the buildings in Devon blue and white is a never-ending job: "You can't even get all the way around before the one you started with needs painting again," Fronheiser says.

The Country Fair buildings are a particular problem. Never designed for permanence, they need constant repair and replacement. Work is done one building at a time so the Village retains the same appearance as the one

built in 1919, except for the thatched roofs which were replaced with shingles long ago. The old trees that make the grounds attractive are the particular enemy of the Village, their roots disrupting the antique piping, the dampness in their shade rotting shingles and framing.

An ever-present danger with half a hundred old wooden buildings is fire. In November of 1952, the row of barns nearest the ring on the east caught fire one night, and several barns were destroyed before the five-alarm fire could be brought under control. A strong wind out of the North prevented barns in the same complex from going up, but carried a sheet of flame all the way across the schooling area to the south barns, where roofs also caught fire. In November, there were no horses in the barns, but fire remains a prevailing nightmare and there are strict rules against smoking in any stable area.

The barns destroyed in the 1952 fire were

129

Horses of the class shown at Devon can expect to be pampered.

Gig's high wheels helped it navigate mud and ruts while the Model T was still Henry Ford's dream.

rebuilt in time for the next show by subscriptions from exhibitors and directors. Subscriptions also built a new twenty-stall barn in 1974–75. The new structure, like most of the old ones, is a "pole barn," its framework and creosoted slabwood shell supported by piles sunk in the ground, rather than by a built-up foundation.

Best of all, Devon has a unity of time, place and character. Ways of doing things, key people and services have developed over the course of eighty years to a point where they have become routine. If everything that goes on in preparation for Devon had to be done for the first time, the show might never take place.

All entry blanks go to the general manager, who determines what horses qualify to show at Devon, based on their records during the preceding year and during the show year until the closing date for entries. Hunter classes are among the most difficult to qualify

everywhere. Three huge tents holding 320 temporary stalls must be set up, jumps and equipment taken out of storage, inspected and repaired, electrical wiring and communications gear installed, provisions laid in for men and horses, booths furnished and stocked, and a million other jobs done before the first visitors arrive. The show office, with Burkholder and Fallon in attendance with several secretaries, is already open. A team of students and alumni, mostly from Westchester State College, does most of the heavy setup work, under a contract with the show. These men also form the "jump crew" during the show itself. They function like a medieval craft guild, choosing their own members. They've been doing the job for as long as anybody can remember and are among the fastest and most efficient in the business. Watching them in the ring is like observing a pit crew at the Indianapolis 500. There's a system for everything.

131

for, because of the large number of entries. Standards are given in the prize list, but they boil down to the unstated requirement that a hunter, to be shown at Devon, must have been champion at one or two A or B-rated shows. (Ratings determined by AHSA, on the basis of prize money and number of classes. Points in an A-rated show count quadruple those in a C-rated show toward individual AHSA point standings). Amateur owners, intermediate and open jumpers qualify on the basis of prize money earned in the previous year. Qualifications for other classes, including those in the junior division, are equally stringent because of the limitations of time, class size and stabling. All of which lends credence to Devon's motto: Where Champions Meet.

Two weeks before the show is scheduled to begin, there is already considerable activity on the grounds. The early spring stillness is broken by the sound of hammering

On Tuesday, the temporary stalls are in place under the canvas and in barns normally used for storage, and the first guests arrive, three days before the junior division begins. These are usually show people, on the road with their horses and so far from home that it is easier to stay on the Devon grounds than to make the trip to the farm and back. Many of them have come from the Lancaster show, about an hour's drive away. They may be planning a campaign of twenty or more shows during the season. Early arrivals may also be trainers and handlers, getting their horses accustomed to the surroundings before the owners arrive just prior to show time. Nearly all of them will be showing in the junior division and will have left the grounds by 8:00 A.M. on the following Sunday morning. Most of the junior horses are stabled under canvas. Exhibitors in other divisions fill up the permanent stabling during junior weekend, and the overflow goes into the tents recently vacated by the juniors. The schooling areas gradually fill up with children, ponies and horses, cantering on the longe line or waiting their turn over the schooling fences.

While the juniors prepare for their big day, a curious transformation is taking place in the Country Village nearby. A procession of delivery vans, cars and trailers, under the supervision of volunteers, salesmen, carpenters, mechanics and interior decorators, is turning it into a combination of elegant boutique and carnival—the Main Line midway, better known as the Devon Country Fair.

Handlers jog their ponies during judging of conformation in a pony roadster class.

Its trainer's attention distracted, a horse on a longe line looks as if it's about to tiptoe off.

11

A Week Down in Devon

The Devon schedule is set up for events each day in every division—hunters, jumpers, Hackneys, fine harness, three-gaited and five-gaited Saddlebreds, and so on. But each day also has its specialty. On Sunday it was the Carriage Marathon; on Memorial Day, the first amateur owner jumping class; and on Tuesday, Operation Goldmine—a drawing for a bracelet of diamonds and gold as a forerunner to Saturday's Devon Derby—and four-in-hand driving.

Devon is the only show in the country with regular competitions for vehicles drawn by four horses, not only exhibits but also tests of driving skill and controllability. They maneuver a figure-eight course, through which the coach must pass at a smart trot between a series of barrels only slightly farther apart than the width of axle, then stop at a designated point.

During the week, nine four-in-hands competed. Mr. and Mrs. James K. Robinson,

Jr. entered a Brewster park coach drawn by four black horses. Mrs. J. Austin Du Pont drove her team of four gray Welsh ponies to a private road coach. Phillip B. Hoffman of Annandale, New Jersey, showed a black and yellow English road coach drawn by four German Holsteiners, a strain originally bred for the artillery. John Fairclough, of Fairview Farm, Newton, New Jersey, showed a road coach with cream-colored door panels, drawn by a team of Canadian crossbreds. Clement R. Hoopes, West Grove, Pennsylvania, exhibited his road coach drawn by a team of purebred Hackneys, as was that of John Cuneo's Hawthorne Melody Farms, Libertyville, Illinois. Susan Saltonstall of Dover, Massachusetts, drove a pony brake behind four Welsh ponies, and Dr. Clarkson Addes of Chester Springs, Pennsylvania, hitched a team of four hunters to his park drag.

Two other unusual driving events had been held earlier—one for open tandems, in

Only 19 more shows to go.

which two horses are hitched one behind the other, won by a pair of Hackneys owned by Mr. and Mrs. Joseph Gendron, Beacon Falls, Connecticut. Another event was held for open unicorns, so named because the hitch has a single leader in front of a pair. The latter was won by a three-horse team from Hawthorne Melody Farms.

The ninth entry in the four-in-hand division, a road coach owned by James Laird of Eel's Foot Farm, West Chester, entered only one class, the speed event for time through an obstacle course, and took second to Clement Hoopes' team. The blue, red and yellow ribbons alternated throughout the week between the entries of Mr. Hoopes, Miss Saltonstall, the Robinsons and Hawthorne Melody Farms, but Hawthorne amassed the most points for the championship awarded Friday night.

The only blue in four-in-hand classes

won during the week by Hawthorne was on Tuesday night, with August A. Busch, Jr. holding the reins. Mr. Busch, a noted whip, is a friend of John Cuneo, the owner of Hawthorne Melody Farms, and recently drove the Hawthorne coach-and-four to a new speed record through the obstacles at the Toronto Winter Fair. Mr. Busch learned how to drive from a German teamster in the days before deliveries were made by truck, and often drives the Anheuser-Busch Clydesdales himself. An all-around horseman, he has also played polo, ridden open jumpers and was MFH of the Bridlespur Hunt Club for more than twenty years. He plans to bring his own four-in-hand to Devon in 1976.

Wednesday is International Day, honoring Canada and Devon's many Canadian exhibitors, and the special event is the police competition. Unfortunately, it is also the evening of the Flyers' victory parade and the

136

Judge in the Carriage Marathon pauses to admire an unusual buggy and its pair of Shetlands.

Devon Carriage Marathon draws more entries than any other event of its type in the U.S.

Putting his best foot forward in an event for American saddlebreds.

Mrs. J. Austin Du Pont and her champion hunter, Gray Ace, on the outside course at Devon in 1930.

Mrs. Edgar Scott winning the ladies' sidesaddle class at Devon in 1953. A leading rider of hunters and the first woman hunter judge at the National Horse Show, Mrs. Scott is now Chairman of the Devon Horse Show Committee.

Philadelphia mounted police are tired out. Still, they put in a good performance as a team and Policeman Richard Levin on Gomer, last year's winner, takes a second to State Police Corporal Francis N. O'Rourke on Asper in the individual competition.

For the plate presented by Richard McDevitt in honor of his father, the Hon. Harry S. McDevitt Challenge Trophy, the individual entry must turn right and left on the forehand, pass right and left, dismount and walk five paces away from the horse, and stand at that distance until the command to mount, then remount and canter to the end of the ring, return at a gallop, stop on command, back up five paces, drop the reins, stand and return to the troop. The most exciting part of the drill is the stop on command from a gallop, forefeet planted and dirt flying; the most difficult is walking away from the horse, which has an uncontrollable de-

sire to follow its rider or rejoin the herd. Most horses alone, with dropped reins, in the middle of a floodlit ring surrounded by thousands of people, can stand it for about ten seconds. The troopers whose horses walked back to the troop when they'd had enough at least had the sympathy of everyone in the exhibitors' stand.

The show moved on. By Volunteers' Day, Thursday, all the entries have had a chance to show what they can do, and the competition for championship in each division has narrowed down to a few leading contenders. The lady's sidesaddle and sidesaddle hunter classes, however, are over and done with on that day. From the size of the class and the interest shown, it seems that there will be more events and even better competition next year, as sidesaddle riding becomes more of a sport and less an exercise in nostalgia.

The winning collection of three Hackneys in 1916, driven by Frank Palmer.

Thursday is also unusual in having an entire morning devoted to breeding classes for yearlings, two-year-olds and three-year-olds. There are classes for thoroughbreds, suitable to become hunters, for "other than thoroughbreds, suitable to become hunters," for mares, suitable to produce hunters, for best Pennsylvania bred yearlings, two-year-olds and three-year-olds, and for young hunters under saddle. The classes are huge—there is no way to qualify entries at the beginning of their careers—but no one would have it any differently. In these classes, you can sense what the old Devon, and the nineteenth century horse fairs that preceded it, must have been like. Many of the entries are local. They have an equal chance with the largest farms for, in the last analysis, no one can tell exactly what a mixture of bloodlines is going to produce. The judges, Steven Hawkins and

Richard Keller, although they know the lineage of many colts and fillies, can only credit the evidence of their eyes.

Take Aim, owned by Mr. and Mrs. Peter Platten of Blue Bell, Pennsylvania, is voted the best young horse, and Limelight, Mrs. Anne Clarke Brady, Afton, Virginia, is reserve. The best Pennsylvania-bred horse is Rippling Charger, Donald F. Cross, Media.

The premiere event of the day, however, is the presentation of an award to Mrs. Clarence J. Lewis, vice president of the Devon Horse Show and Country Fair, for fifty years of devoted service.

Friday is Bicentennial Day; City and National Park Service representatives present trophies, and everyone settles back to watch the USET open jumping class.

Friday is also the day on which the Tack Room Awards are presented. If you want to see the tack rooms, it is best to have a friend

140

Miss Joan Fletcher shows her champion American saddlebred, Little Colonel, in 1942.

Railbirds' favorite Rodney Jenkins gets the most out of every horse he rides.

Rider applies direct rein (right) while still in the air to put a hunter on the best line for the next fence.

DEVON
HORSE SHOW
DEVON, PA.

Six-In-Hand at Devon Horse Show 1912

Desk blotters once advertised the show. This one pictures a six-in-hand of Hackneys.

May 28, 29, 30, 31,
Ladies' Day, May 31

Devon's jump crew is one of the fastest in the show world.

who is also an exhibitor or an official to guide you through the stable area. The general public is not prohibited from wandering through the barns and savoring the real atmosphere of Devon, but horses kick and dogs bite. To anyone unaccustomed to all the quirks of genus equus and his handlers, the trip can be an embarrassing obstacle course. If you can get an escorted tour, by all means do so. The tack rooms of the major stables are latter-day facsimiles of the satin pavilions set up in the field by knights in King Arthur's time: dimly lit silken caves filled with gleaming harness and hung about with trophies. They are for show. As far as I know, no one has ever been seen sitting on the matching camp chairs inside or planning strategy around the round table. The blankets with the farm name are freshly laundered and stay that way all week.

The Final Hours

Saturday, Championship Day, the day of the major challenge trophies and the big stakes classes, dawns threateningly and stays that way all day long. Except for the local working hunter section, which goes on and on forever in the Gold Ring, in divisions of fifty, most of the classes are smaller, the result of constant elimination during the preceding week.

Everything is on schedule. The rain has held off. It is the second jump-off of the $5000 open jumper stakes. Antar and Rodney Jenkins have just put in their last, fast clean round when the first drops begin to fall.

The jump crew scrambles to clear a space for the Devon Derby drawing and the words that will close the show for the year. The wire squirrel cage containing the Devon Derby tickets is rushed to the ring in a pickup truck and unloaded as the Bryn Mawr Hospital nurses in their starched uniforms descend from the committee stand to make the drawing. It begins to rain harder; lightning flashes and thunder rumbles. Those who feel themselves born unlucky head for the gates. As soon as the last number has been called, in a lull between showers, the heavens open in a true Devon deluge. The throng that had jammed every available inch around the ring vanishes into the night's traffic jam. Philosophical van drivers shut off their engines and wait for things to clear. They'll load the horses in the morning.

In the committee stand the directors rehash the show, already making plans for next year. In the press box next door, wrapup stories are being written and phoned or telexed in for tomorrow's edition. The last entries are being made in the sacred marked program that contains the show's entire results. The publicity staff is trying to decide where to go for a party.

At 12:30, the guards open the gates for official cars. The ring, in spite of its new drainage system, gleams like a dark pool under the darkened floodlights. On the walkways of the Country Fair, the flood carries away the accumulated debris of 40,000 people. Wilmer Fronheiser and his crew will be able to clean up, dismantle and make the necessary repairs in about two weeks.

The committee stand closes. The lights go off in the press box and the man with the key turns it in the lock, descends the stairs and plods off with an air of fatalism through ankle-deep water. Devon is over for another year.

It is still alive in the barns, warm and steaming, and will be until the last horse is loaded. The next stop is Ox Ridge, Connecticut. Good show! We'll be back!

145